Devbhoomi Uttarakhand

PRAISE FOR DEVBHOOMI UTTARAKHAND

Dear Ms Neha Mittal,

Thank you for sending your beautiful book on Uttarakhand to me. I am sure it will find many readers. My best wishes and please continue writing about our mountain state.

—Ruskin Bond, Award-winning Author

A visually stunning book. Each page tells a story of our rich Pahadi culture, capturing the essence of the land that holds a special place in my heart. A must-read for everyone eager to discover the cultural richness that defines our Uttarakhand.

—Jubin Nautiyal, Playback Singer

Neha Mittal's *Devbhoomi Uttarakhand* fills a significant gap by bringing the cultural richness of the mountain state onto the literary map. Through meticulous research and interesting narratives, Mittal makes the diverse cultures of Uttarakhand come alive. The book's use of colourful illustrations, maps, and images enhances the storytelling, offering readers an immersive journey into the sacred landscapes of Uttarakhand. Whether you are a history buff, a nature lover or simply someone in search of understanding the vibrant cultures of Uttarakhand, the book is sure to leave you enlightened and enriched.

—Lt Gen Gurmit Singh, Hon'ble Governor, Uttarakhand, PVSM, UYSM, AVSM, VSM (Retd)

Devbhoomi Uttarakhand: The Fascinating Culture of the Central Himalaya is an eminently readable and wonderfully illustrated collection of twelve offerings from debut author Neha Mittal, a young civil servant who was inspired by the picturesque settings of her training institutions at Mussoorie and Shimla. Fortuitously for her, as well as the readers of this book, her first job was also in the Himalaya. From the origin stories of the four Dhams to the splendid descriptions of alpine traders, the indigenous tribes of Terai and Nanda Devi, the mountain goddess, and oracle kings, Neha also tells us about bugyals, forests, man-eaters, and hunters in a narrative that draws multiple sources and blends history with legend. The text is embellished with pictures which nudge the readers to form a visual imprint in their minds and the maps are a spur to travel on routes that are both enchanting and challenging.

—Shri Sanjeev Chopra, IAS (retd), Festival Director, Valley of Words

It's a wonderful book. Well-researched and well-written, it gives the reader a very deep peep into our Devbhoomi Uttarakhand. The best part of the book is the illustrations, pictures and maps that make the book a visual delight to the readers. The book also gives readers a good insight into the Char Dham circuit and various local tribes and communities of Uttarakhand.

—Shri Ashok Kumar, Former DGP Uttarakhand

Neha Mittal's *Devbhoomi Uttarakhand* unveils the cultural tapestry of Uttarakhand with meticulous research and captivating narratives. Through engaging storytelling, vibrant illustrations and insightful visuals, Neha takes us on a journey into the diverse cultures of Uttarakhand, offering readers an immersive experience of its sacred landscapes. Whether you are a seasoned traveller or a curious enthusiast of Himalayan culture, this book promises to enrich your understanding and appreciation of the region's rich heritage.

—Anoop Nautiyal, Founder, Social Development for Communities (SDC) Foundation

Devbhoomi Uttarakhand

THE FASCINATING CULTURES OF THE CENTRAL HIMALAYA

NEHA MITTAL

NU VOICE PRESS

NU VOICE

First published by NU VOICE PRESS 2023
An imprint of Hubhawks Pvt. Ltd
www.nuvoicepress.com

This edition published by NU VOICE PRESS 2024

ISBN: 978-81-963184-8-2

Typeset by Saanvi Graphics, Noida
Printed at Nutech Print Services - India
Published by Nu Voice Press

To my family without whose support this book would not have seen the light of the day.

CONTENTS

PART C

HIMALAYA: THE SHADES OF NATURE

FOREWORD

The state of Uttarakhand, made of principal regions of Garhwal and Kumaon, is an ancient land with a cultural history that is not only complex but also interwoven in its oral traditions.

Cultural history of the Uttarakhand region has been written about in the past but, in my opinion, has suffered from two lacunae. Firstly, they have failed to look at commonalities within Uttarakhand's social groups, creating binaries of Garhwali-Kumaoni, mountain-valley, *khas*-indigenous etc., while attempting to describe particularities of mountain communities living in different valleys carved by Uttarakhand's great rivers. Secondly, the insistence upon material and textual evidence has prevented academics from looking at the oral traditions of the region, which continue to be critical records of history while being such an integral part of current social life.

This book breaches both barriers and adopts a multi-disciplinary approach to writing a cultural history of Uttarakhand, a region that, even though going back into the dawn of the human age, became a separate state only in the year 2000.

When the author approached me about her intentions of undertaking such a monumental task, I was a little apprehensive. However, her perseverance seems to have paid off in this lucid and illustrated account that weaves aspects of geography, myth and folklore into a gripping historical narrative of Uttarakhand.

During the course of this work, the author has gathered fascinating insights into the region's past. For instance, she refers to the general acceptance of river Alaknanda the main source of the venerable Ganga in Puranic literature until colonial surveyors took it upon themselves to grant this merit to river Bhagirathi. Then, owing largely to British occupation the capital of Garhwal shifted from Srinagar to Tehri, and the Dham of Gangotri gained recognition due to its proximity to Gaumukh, the source of river Bhagirathi traced by colonial expeditionists. Such insights make for interesting reading.

The book should be of interest to those looking to understand Uttarakhand and its past through the lens of orality. It offers a deep perspective on the archive while delving into how geography has dictated the cultural and social practices in the region. A project of this nature, which describes the sacred geography of Uttarakhand, tracing its links all the way to our ancient scriptures, is both timely and welcome.

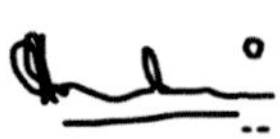

–Lokesh Ohri (*Anthropologist*)

POLITICAL MAP OF UTTARAKHAND*

** Created by Science Mapping services*

INTRODUCTION

As the dew is dried up by the morning sun, so are the sins of humankind by the sight of the snows of the Himalaya.

– *Skanda Purana*[1]

Running over an east-west axis for 2400 kilometres, the Himalaya is the world's youngest and most dynamic mountain range. Home to 144 peaks measuring above 7,000 metres, 14 over 8,000 metres, the Himalaya have been considered sacred in Indian civilization for thousands of years. In Hinduism, the Himalaya is personified as Himaraja, the king of mountains and father-in-law of Lord Shiva. The snowy summits are also where Lord Shiva engages in meditation, and where events of great cosmological significance like the descent of Ganga from heaven have occurred. Within the Himalayan region, the place believed to be the most holy is Uttarakhand, popularly known by the epithet, Devbhoomi, "the sacred land of Gods".

What makes this region so special? The best explanation comes from Shanti Parva of the great epic *Mahabharata* when King Yudhishthira asks the Kuru patriarch Bhishma, "Which countries and mountains are the foremost in terms of sanctity?" Bhishma replies, "Those countries and mountains should be regarded as being foremost in sanctity through which flows the foremost of all rivers—Ganga. Those countries and points of the compass that are destitute of the sacred waters of Ganga are like nights without the moon or like trees without flowers."[2]

The belief in the purifying and nourishing powers of Ganga has been a part of the Hindu psyche since ancient times. River Ganga, which is believed to originate in heaven, embodies holiness against which the sacredness of other religious sites is measured. Drinking and bathing in Ganga not only physically cleans the body, but also symbolically cleanses the soul by washing away all the sins and subsequently facilitates one's entry into heaven. In the *Mahabharata*, it is remarked that, "As *Amrit* (ambrosia) is to the Gods, as *Swadha* (offerings) is to the *Pitris* (ancestors), even so is Ganga water to human beings. Hundreds of sacrifices cannot produce that merit which men of restrained souls are capable of acquiring by bathing in the sacred waters of Ganga."

The belief in its supernatural properties and its descent from heaven prompted generations of travellers, ascetics and pilgrims to trace the river to its celestial origins. Naturally, it led them deep into the formidable Himalaya, whose snowy peaks soaring above the clouds seemed to penetrate the vaults of heaven. This further cemented the belief that Himalaya act as conduit between Earth and heaven. In their desire to be in communion with Gods or to gain liberation from their worldly existence, these adventurous pilgrims set up hermitage along the banks of Ganga and its tributaries. The new inhabitants were *rishis, charanas* and *siddhas*[3] who engaged in a daily ritual of sacrifices and yoga and further purified the environment. They ended up attracting many other visitors including exiled royal princes, renunciants and even supernatural beings like Yakshas, Gandharvas, Apsarasas, and Vidyadharas. Among these, the most celebrated hermitage was Badrikashram, or Badrinath, founded by the divine duo Nara and Narayana at the mouth of the holy Alaknanda (one of the tributaries of Ganga). The venerated site forms the backdrop of many memorable adventures of Pandavas when they visit the hermitage during their years of exile in the *Mahabharata.*

Apart from holy hermitages, the pristine terrain of the Himalaya came to be viewed as infused with divine presence, such as that of Lord Shiva in snowy fields of Kedarnath or his different manifestations at sites collectively called *Panch Kedar*. With time, as more and more people settled in the general vicinity, each lake, peak, meadow came to be inscribed with a sacred meaning, ultimately contributing in the formation of a 'sacred geography' that we know today as 'Devbhoomi Uttarakhand'. Although home to innumerable holy sites, a group of *tirthas,* (the sacred spaces) called the Himalayan Char-Dham are the most popular religious attraction of present times. Open for just six months, the pilgrimage circuit encompasses the most visited places of Uttarakhand – the shrines of Badrinath, Kedarnath, Gangotri and Yamunotri. As per the figures of Uttarakhand Tourism Department, around 40 lakh people visited the religious circuit, with Badrinath recording the highest footfall of around 15.25 lakh and Yamunotri the lowest of 4.73 lakh in 2022[4]. Situated in the rugged heart of the Greater Himalayan range, the story of their evolution as the most sacred tirthas of Hinduism, using references from mythology, history and travelogues, is explored in great detail in Part-A of the book.

The Himalayas are not geographically homogenous, rather, they constitute a remarkably diverse topography. The lofty mountains can be subdivided into three successive ranges – the Greater Himalaya, the Lesser Himalaya, and the Outer Himalaya, all three of varying heights and separated from each other by fault lines. Altitude mimics latitude such that when we climb a few kilometre, the climate and landscape change profoundly, mirroring the travel through latitude. One astonishing example of this is the fact that the average temperatures drop by more than six degrees celsius for every kilometre climbed. This results in a variety of habitats in a relatively concentrated region, ranging from cold deserts, alpine meadows and temperate forests to subtropical wilderness. This gets reflected in the cultural diversity of the state of Uttarakhand.

Culture, in its most profound sense, refers to a system of beliefs and lifestyle developed by a community in response to its surroundings. In Uttarakhand, the Himalayan geography has played a significant role in shaping the culture of its people. The cold desert of Trans-Himalaya is home to the nomadic Bhotia community who not only survived but thrived in the harsh terrain with their well-adapted cultural practices. Similarly, the dreaded sub-tropical forests of Terai, full of hostile marshes and malaria, became the home of Tharu and Boksa tribes. Once the tallest peak in India, Mount Nanda Devi (7,816 meters) stands tall in its formidable sanctuary. But, for the people of Garhwal, the mountain embodies their dear daughter Goddess Nanda, who lives in the sanctuary with her husband Lord Shiva. In the Nanda Devi Raj Jat, celebrated every twelve years, people undertake a long and arduous journey through villages, forests, meadows, and frozen lakes to ritually enact Nanda's journey from her *mait* (natal home) to her *sasural* (husband's home) on Mount Kailash. Thus, geography not only shapes the culture of communities as in the case of Bhotias and Tharus, but itself gets shaped when rich cultural meanings are inscribed upon it by people like in the case of Nanda Devi. Nature and culture form a complex link which is observable to some degree in all the communities of the state, and has been explored in Part-B of the book.

Culture in any given place is never static but dynamic, ever changing in response to internal churn and external influences. The most significant external influence that dramatically impacted the region's culture was the coming of the East India Company following the Anglo-Gurkha war in 1815. Their arrival marked the commencement of an era of surveying, mapping and exploring the hitherto uncharted length and breadth of the Himalayan terrain to gain better control of the region, and to satisfy the urge to know the unknown. In the time that followed, some of the highest peaks of Garhwal and Kumaon were measured, the sources of river Ganga and Yamuna were traced, and hidden gems like the Valley of Flowers were brought to attention of the outside world. However, the need to control nature and use it for economic benefits led to the introduction to new ways of scientific management and incessant exploitation of forests and wildlife. In some places, modern interventions transformed the landscape beyond recognition, like in the foothills of the Terai which led to bumper revenue at the cost of marginalisation of vulnerable local communities. The short-sighted policies of colonial era continued after the independence, until agitation by locals, and large-scale disasters—the latest being the sinking of Joshimath town 2023—forced the government to rethink its policy and take into view the fragility of the Himalaya and their capacity to sustain relentless human intervention. The history of resource management and the conflict between the colonial extraction approach rooted in revenue generation which continues till today, and the native 'sacred' approach based on community participation and management, is explored in Part-C of the book, through the story of Uttarakhand's meadows, forests, and wildlife.

After my posting in Uttarakhand and multiple trips throughout the state, I became aware of the dearth of good books that explored the different facets of Pahadi culture in sufficient depth and an engaging style. The available texts oscillated between two extremes of a spectrum; there were either jargon-laden, difficult to understand research papers or simple tourist guidebooks containing long lists of places to visit. This book grew from my desire to fill this gap and convey the state's rich and diverse cultures holistically. During my research, I observed that the culture of Uttarakhand or 'Pahad' is not only lively and vibrant but also very closely integrated with its Himalayan setting in unique ways. Hence, this became the common theme of my book – exploring each cultural facet through a multi-disciplinary lens, which included, mythology, history, geography, economy, and kinship.

For this book, I consulted multiple sources. The list includes three volumes of the Himalayan Gazetteers and other records of the colonial period, research papers, books, news articles, interviews with experts, and field visits to weave together a well-rounded and well-researched narrative. Wherever required, I have also used local folklore and the *Mahabharata* to corroborate many standard sources of historiography including inscriptions and documented records. I have tried to keep the book as simple as possible, and made use of illustrations, photos and maps to convey the information better.

I hope that readers, especially the youth, find this book useful for learning about the fascinating cultural diversity found in the state and how the majestic Himalaya forms an inseparable part of its communities.

PART A

CHAR-DHAM: A SACRED GEOGRAPHY

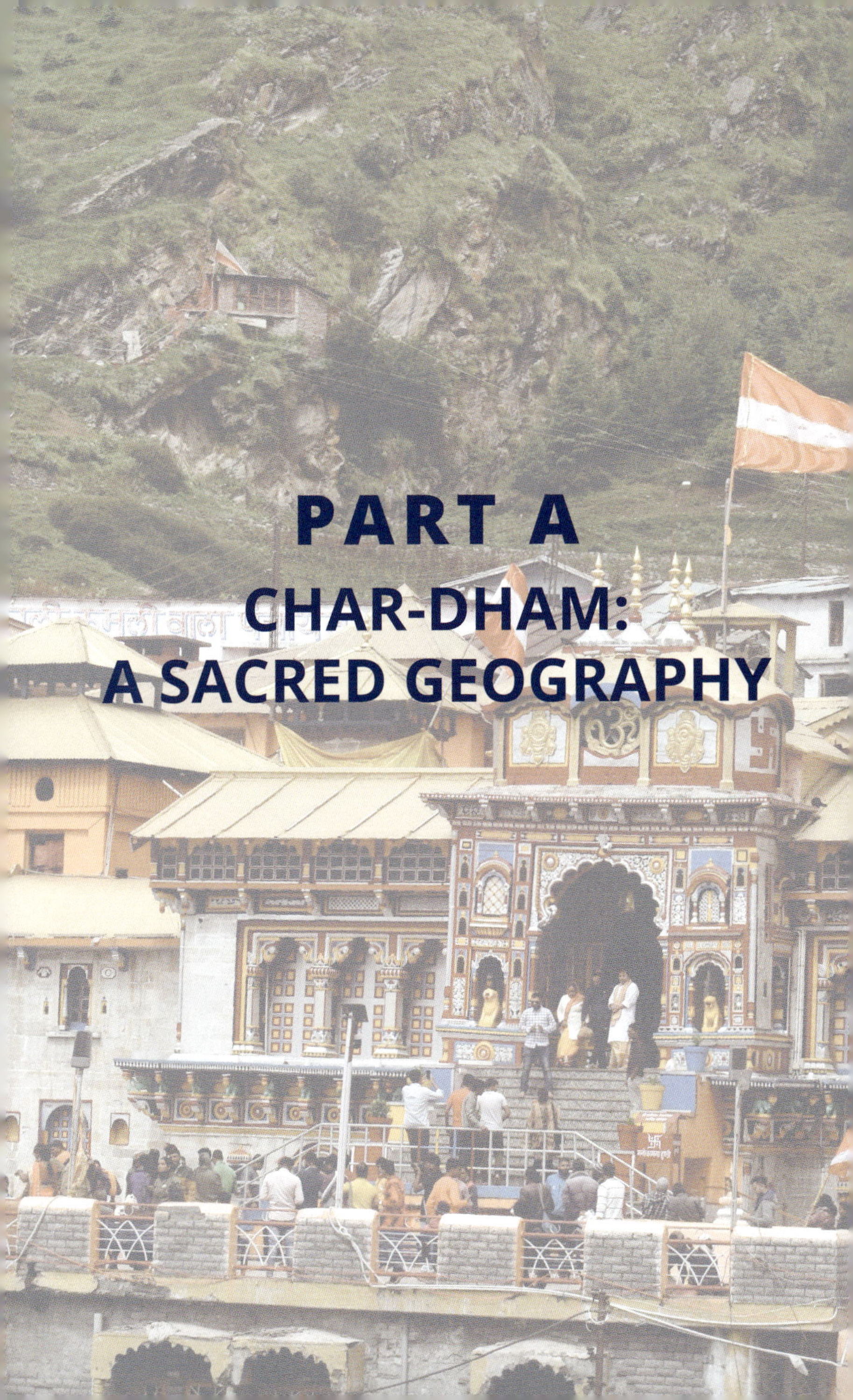

1

BADRINATH: WHERE DWELLS NARAYANA

One day Garuda, the divine bird and vehicle of Lord Vishnu, visited his old friend, the Sage Galava.[5] He found Galava in a state of despair. Upon further enquiry, he found that Galava had been asked by his guru, Vishwamitra, for eight hundred horses as *guru dakshina* (teacher's fees to be paid by student upon completion of studies), with the condition that they should be pure and white as the moon except for one of their ears, which should be black.

Galava did not know where to find such unusual horses. Garuda reassured his friend, promising to help him with his predicament. Boasting his knowledge of the four directions, he asked Galava which direction he wanted to go towards first. Curious at Garuda's boast, Galava asked his friend to regale him with tales of all the enchanting, magical places he had seen in the east, the south and the west. At last, he asked Garuda to tell him about the wonders of the north, and the lord of the birds said, 'O Galava, the abode of all treasures of the north is the Himalaya, stretching in a line from east to west.' And then, Garuda described the holiest tirthas of the Himalaya, the presence of which makes the direction the most superior of all.

Garuda said, 'Here is the place of Badri, where eternally dwells Krishna, Narayana's self and Nara, the most exalted of all male beings.'[6] The sages Nara and Narayan are closely connected with the Hindu epic *Mahabharata*. Pandavas, the heroes of the epic, lose their kingdom to the Kauravas in the infamous game of dice where their wife Draupadi is humiliated. As per the ensuing deal with Kauravas, the Pandavas need to spend twelve years in exile in a forest and another year incognito to get their kingdom back.

When the Pandavas are in the forest, Sage Vyas visits their hermitage. He advises Yudhishthira to prepare for war in case Duryodhana refuses to honour his promise after the end of their exile. Bereft of any allies or wealth, the Pandavas would lose the war. Yudhishthira should give Arjuna the task of obtaining an array of celestial weapons by appeasing Indra and tilt the balance in their favour. Yudhishthira instructs Arjuna to perform penance and acquire the divine weapons from Indra. Armed with his sword and bow Gandiva, Arjuna heads north, towards the majestic Himalaya.

While crossing the Himalaya, he is stopped by an old ascetic who implores him to shun his weapons as the Himalaya is the holy land and weapons are not required there. On Arjuna's refusal, the ascetic reveals himself to be Indra in disguise. He advises Arjuna to propitiate Shiva, after

Figure 1 Arjuna-Kirata during their standoff

which Indra will give him the weapons he seeks. Ascending the Himalaya, he finds a suitable spot on the banks of the Ganga, near the holy hermitage of Badri and begins his terrible penance. To test Arjuna's resolve, Shiva assumes the guise of Kirata, the hunter, and arrives at Arjuna's place with his party of attendants called Ganas. At the same time, a demon called Muka with a desire to kill Arjuna, takes the form of a boar and charges towards him. When Arjuna aims his arrow at the angry boar coming towards him, Kirata calls to him to stop. Arjuna ignores him. They both hit the boar at the same time, who dies on the spot. Arjuna and Kirata trade heated remarks, and both stake a claim to the animal while accusing the other of engaging in improper conduct. The matter escalates into a fight. Arjuna showers Kirata with a volley of arrows but it has no effect on the hunter. Arjuna's quiver, given to him by Agni, soon runs out of the arrows. He then uses his bow Gandiva to hit Kirata, but the latter seizes it and throws it away. Enraged, Arjuna strikes the hunter with his sword, which breaks on impact with his body. With no weapons left, the duo engages in fist fights, and Kirata's severe blows render Arjuna unconscious.

When he regains consciousness, Shiva gives him divine sight, enabling Arjuna to witness Kirata's true form. Feeling ashamed and humbled, he seeks forgiveness for his transgression. Shiva, aware of the purpose of his penance, is pleased with him. He presents Arjuna with *Pashupatastra*, a terrible weapon capable of great destruction. In the process, he also makes Arjuna aware of his former birth. It turns out that Arjuna is the reincarnation of the Sage Nara who, along with his companion Narayana, had performed penance at the hermitage of Badri for aeons. His friend and mentor, Krishna, is the reincarnation of Narayana, and both had taken birth in this mortal world to remove the unrighteousness plaguing it. After obtaining the required weapons from Shiva, Indra appears before Arjuna. As promised earlier, he leads Arjuna to heaven to teach him the use of celestial weapons.

While Arjuna is busy with Indra, the other Pandavas spend their time in the company of holy sages and ascetics, listening to their discourses, and engaging in philosophical discussions. Sage Dhaumya advises them to spend their time in exile wisely and counsels them on the merits of undertaking pilgrimages. Motivated by Dhaumya's advice, the Pandavas undertake an extensive pilgrimage circuit across the length and breadth of the Indian subcontinent. As years pass, Arjuna sends Sage Lomasha to convey the news of his well-being to his brothers who, by this time, are anxious to see their beloved sibling. With the desire to meet Arjuna, the Pandavas and Draupadi start their journey towards the Himalaya. With Lomasha as their guide, the entourage reaches Gangadwar (modern Haridwar). Looking at the towering mountains ahead, Lomasha addresses the Pandavas, and describes in great detail about the sacred Himalaya and their destination.

"O' King! These mountains are beautiful and sacred. On their lofty heights is the region of Mount Gandhamadana, frequented by the siddhas, rishis and other immortals. There lies the sacred hermitage of Badri, where the eternally present Nara and Narayana perform their penance. That holy abode is inaccessible to the common man. Only those who firmly observe their vows and perform austerities could reach the place. Those who are not in control of their senses encounter various difficulties. Therefore, let us live only on roots and fruits, and be restrained in our conduct so that we reach our destination safely."

Preparing their minds and keeping strict vigil, the Pandavas start their journey. Within a few days, they reach the kingdom of Kunindas. Subahu, the lord of the kingdom, is pleased to see them. Knowing that the road ahead is rugged and uneven, the Pandavas leave their cooks and chariots in care of Subahu and resume their travel. As they venture further, they encounter a violent storm. The sky grows dark, strong winds uproot the trees from the ground and a heavy downpour follows. Shivering in cold, the party spends the night battling the storm.

When the dawn breaks, the storm subsides, and, they resume their journey towards Badrikashram. They travel a short distance when Draupadi suddenly faints. After she regains consciousness, Yudhishthira asks Bhima, "O' Bhima, we have to cross many mountains. They will be of uneven terrain, covered with ice and difficult to walk upon. How will Draupadi cross them?" Bhima thinks for a while, then replies, "I can carry Draupadi. But considering the difficulty

Figure 2 Pandavas at Badrika-ashrama with the Badri tree in the backdrop

of this route and the increasing possibility of encounters with dangerous beings ahead, it would be better if I summon my son, Ghatotkacha." Bhima remembers his son, who appears instantly with his band of fellow demons. Together, they hoist the party onto their backs and travel through the sky.

Looking down through the clouds, the Himalaya looks mesmerising. The Pandavas take in the mountains, foothills, rivers and dense forests populated by birds and a variety of animals. After passing through many such pleasant places, they finally spot the ancient hermitage of Nara-Narayana. At its centre stood a huge Badri (Jujube tree) called Vishala, after which the hermitage had been named. The gigantic tree with its thick round trunk was a deep shade of brown, full of dense foliage, wide sprawling branches with holy fruits, dripping with honey, and inhabited by an assortment of birds. Having reached Badri at last, the Pandavas are warmly received by the pious ascetics and maharishis who live there.

The tirtha of Badrinath, known by many names such as Badri, Badrika or Badrikashram, is one of the holiest tirtha frequently mentioned and venerated in *Mahabharata*. This is because Arjuna and Krishna, the prime heroes of the epic, were the reincarnation of Sage Nara and Narayana, who reincarnated to relieve the Earth from the burden of unrighteousness. Symbolically, Nara represents the enlightened human soul who has achieved eternal companionship with Narayana, the supreme God, a goal yearned for by all devotees. The two sages are given an exalted status in the *Mahabbharata*, so much so that the epic opens with an invocation to them—

> "Om! Having bowed down to Narayana and Nara, the most exalted male being, and also to the Goddess Saraswati, must the word Jaya be uttered."[7]

Because of the importance accorded to Nara-Narayana in *Mahabbharata*, their hermitage at Badri is described by the best of sages including Lomashaand Dhaumya, as the 'foremost of all holy spots'.[8] Located on the banks of Ganga (Alaknanda), the hermitage got its name from the Badri tree which was the chief marker of the place. According to local folklore, when Lord Narayana first started meditating on this spot, his consort Lakshmi got worried for his well-being. She took the form of a huge Badri tree to protect her husband from the piercing sunlight, violent winds and biting cold common to this region. The hermitage became known as Badrinath, or Lord of Badri, the form assumed by Lakshmi, of whom Narayana was the lord.[9]

Today, Badrinath is visited by lakhs of people every year, either as a part of the Char-Dham circuit or as a standalone journey. Akin to the Pandavas in the story above, the pilgrims start their journey from Haridwar or Gangadwar, the place where Ganga descends from the mountains and starts her

Figure 3 Map showing the pilgrimage route to Badrinath along river Ganga

journey through the plains. Taking a dip in one of the many famous ghats, the pilgrim readies himself to sojourn in the mountains, appearing as an unbroken wall in the north.

The journey is along the banks of the Ganga, tracing its path upwards. At Devprayag, 96 kilometres upstream of Haridwar, two major tributaries, the turquoise-coloured Alaknanda and blue-hued Bhagirathi, coming from separate directions, unite to form the Ganga. After bathing in the sacred *sangam* (confluence), the pilgrim moves along river Alaknanda to reach Srinagar, the principal city of Garhwal, which had served as the royal capital of Garhwal kings during the medieval period. Its location was ideal for human settlement as it was a broad and fertile valley. The valley was populated by Kuninda tribe when the Pandavas visited this place, a fact that indicates the antiquity of its occupation.[10]

Continuing along the route, the modern pilgrim passes Rudraprayag, where Alaknanda receives the waters of Mandakini coming down from Kedarnath, and after travelling hundred kilometres upstream arrives in Joshimath. Previously known as Jyotirmath or the monastery of light, the town grew around the *matha* (monastery) which was established by the renowned religious reformer, Adi Shankaracharya to propagate Advaita Vedanta doctrine to the masses. The place was selected primarily for its proximity to Badrinath and its ability to support year-round habitation even in winter. Today, nested in a dense network of narrow alleys, the matha still exists but the seat of the head lies empty. The position of the head was hotly contested after the death of last pontiff, Brahmananda Saraswati in 1953, and since then, it has been mired in legal battles. Within the premises are two caves, one said to be used by Shankaracharya himself for meditation and the other by his disciple, Totakcharya. Close by is a two-storey Narsimha temple, in the lower courtyard of which is a small hall. An empty seat called Shankaracharya Gaddi is kept, where the ascetic would hold discussions with his disciples. It is believed that Shankaracharya placed Totakcharya in charge of this matha and proceeded alone towards Kedarnath.

The Badrinath temple is situated 45 kilometres north of Joshimath on the banks of Alaknanda. Apart from being a part of Himalayan Char-Dham circuit—Badrinath,

Figure 4 Badrinath temple

Kedarnath, Gangotri and Yamunotri—Badrinath is also apart of the older, pan-Indian and original circuit of Char-Dham established by Shankaracharya. In ninth century CE, Shankaracharya had undertaken an expedition across the length and breadth of the Indian subcontinent and established one Dham in four cardinal directions. Badrinath is the northernmost Dham of this circuit. When Shankaracharya visited the place, the Badri tree marking the tirtha had disappeared. While bathing in Alaknanda, he spotted an idol of Narayana in the nearby sulphur pool of Tapta Kund and consecrated the image in a nearby cave.

During the reign of Panwar dynasty, founded in fourteenth century, the image was shifted from the cave and established in the sanctum of the temple constructed by the king in vernacular architecture. Dedicated to Lord Badrinath, also called Narayana and Vishnu, the colourful facade of the temple painted in rich hues of gold, red and blue stands in stark contrast to the pale mountainous background. The image of Narayana, depicted in a seated posture, is made of the sacred Shaligram stone. However, only its face is visible as it is covered with layers of clothes and ornaments. The statue is surrounded by the images of Kubera (Lord of Wealth), Uddhava (friend and counsellor of Badri's incarnation Krishna), sages Nara, Narayana and Narada, the celestial devotee of Lord. Only the chief priest called Rawal is allowed inside the shrine and only he can touch the image of Badri. The post of Rawal has been traditionally held by Namboothiri Brahmins hailing from the southern state of Kerala. This practice is believed to have been established by Shankaracharya since he was a native of that state. The Rawal is assisted in his duties by the local Dimri Brahmins who follow his instructions and carry on with the daily *pooja* (worship), *paath* (public recital of scriptures) and preparation of *prasad* (a food offering made to a god).

The temple consists of two sections beside the sanctum, the *darshan mandapa* (where daily rituals are conducted) and the outer *sabha mandapa,* where devotees gather to get *darshan* (beholding) of the lord. Hot springs abound the region and the water from one such spring is channelled to form *kunds* (bathing pools)—notably Tapta Kund and Narad Kund which are used by the pilgrims to bathe and purify themselves before entering the temple. Taking a dip in the lukewarm water of the pools not only provides comfort from the cold weather but much needed refreshment for the pilgrims weary from distant travels. Flanking the temple are two mountains called Nara Parvat and Narayan Parvat, on whose summit Nara and Narayana are said to be engaged in deep penance, invisible to the eyes of mortal humans.

Badrinath is another name of Lord Vishnu, who, as per the Hindu cosmology, assumes the role of preserver, and maintains world order. The same function is performed by monarchy on Earth where they are expected to maintain law and order and protect their subjects. It is of little wonder that many Hindu kings of the past have sought legitimacy by associating themselves with Narayana, the lord and preserver of the universe. Lord Badrinath was the state deity of the Kingdom of Garhwal, and later, of the Kingdom of Tehri (after British annexation). The Garhwal kings were considered representative of Badrinath on Earth, and were conferred the title of 'Bolanda Badri' or 'through whom Lord Badri speaks'.

After independence the kingdom merged with the Indian state, but the importance of the royal family to Badrinath remained indispensable and they continue to play a significant role in the most important rituals of the temple—the closing and opening of the *kapats* (gates).

Diwali, the festival of lights, celebrated in late October or early November (as per the Hindu calendar), marks the beginning of winters in North India. For Badrinath, located at a height of 3300 metres, it is time for Lord Badri to retire to his winter seat. As the wind becomes chillier and light snow starts falling, preparations begin to close the gates of Dham. The Bhotia maidens of Mana, the last village on the India-China border, skilfully weave fine wool obtained from mountain goats into warm blankets for Lord Badri. The blankets are dipped in ghee prepared from the milk of Pahadi cows. The image of the Lord standing in the temple sanctum is laid in a supine position, and the blankets woven by Bhotia maidens are wrapped around the image. A big lamp is lit in front of the shrine, which continues to burn for the next six months. Known as the *akhand jyoti* (the eternal flame), it is believed that lucky are those devotees who can catch a glimpse of the flame when the gates open the following year. The gates themselves are secured with three locks and different authorities are entrusted with their keys. One key is given to the Rajguru of the royal family from the Nautiyal community. Two other keys are each left with the representatives of the Mehta community and of the Bhandari community, both residing in Pandukeshwar, the winter seat of Lord Badri. The *chal murti* (mobile image) of Kubera, the treasurer of Lord Badri and that of Uddhava, considered to be *pratinidhi* (representative) of Lord Badri, are placed inside the richly decorated palanquin and taken with much fanfare to the small hamlet of Pandukeshwar.

Located 23 kilometres downstream on the bank of Alaknanda, Pandukeshwar is named after King Pandu, the father of Pandavas, who is believed to have obtained his five sons here and also met his death in this locality. The antiquity of the place is attested by the discovery of four copper plate inscriptions dating back to the ninth century which sheds light on the political and cultural environment of their time. The inscriptions were discovered in the Yog Dhyan Badri temple complex, which also serves as the winter seat for the image of Kubera and Uddhava brought down from Badrinath. The *gaddi* (seat) and staff of Shankaracharya are also taken out during closing ceremony and placed in Narsingh temple at Joshimath. With the closing of the temple, the town and the surrounding villages also migrate with their livestock to their respective winter dwellings. The temple priests retire to Joshimath while the Rawal returns to his native place in Kerala. It is believed that Lord Badri is worshipped for six months by humans and for another six months by sage Narada at Badrinath. When the winter arrives with full force, and the town is covered under thick layers of snow, sage Narada engages himself in worshipping Lord Badri on behalf of all the Gods of cosmos.

The following year, in early May, on the auspicious date of Akshay Tritiya, the gates of Dham are opened. It is a significant event for entire Garhwal, especially for the royal family. The royal palace at Narendranagar becomes abuzz with preparations. The Dimri Brahmins, who have traditionally served as priests to Badrinath and belong to the *Dimri Panchayat Pratinidhi*, arrive in the palace and conduct pooja of Narayana as ordained by the customs. The Maharani (Queen), along with other married ladies, dressed in auspicious yellow clothes, performs the ritual of '*tilon ka til pirona*' where oil is manually extracted from sesame(*til*) seeds. The extracted oil is used for the first *abhishek* (consecration) of Lord Badri, after the Dham opens. *Kalash* (pots) are filled with the freshly pressed oil and taken by the Dimri Brahmins for the gate opening ceremony. The chief priest or Rawal also returns from Kerala and arrives at Pandukeshwar to where images of Uddhava and Kubera are lavishly decorated in a palanquin and taken to Badrinath by the followers on foot.

The auspicious time to open the gates arrives during Brahma muhurta, the last quarter of the night, which begins from 3:40 A.M. and lasts till 48 minutes before sunrise. Amidst the chanting of Vedic mantras and shouts of *Jai Badri Vishal*, the kapats open after an interval of six months. The Rawal enters the temple and establishes Kubera and Uddhava in their positions in the sanctum. The image of Narayana is placed in its original position and the blankets removed are distributed among devotees as prasad. The oil-filled pots brought from the royal court are handed over to the Rawal by Dimri Brahmins who performs the abhishek of Lord Badri. Temple is then declared open to receive devotees who travel from all over India to obtain a darshan of Lord Badri. The temple remains open until Diwali when the gates are closed and this cycle continues every year.

For the ancient Indians, Badrinath was one of the holiest places of the Earth. The presence of Narayana and Nara was the contributing factor in elevating the place as a tirtha. However, the primary reason which prompted Nara-Narayan to set their hermitage at the spot was its location near the source of river Ganga. As per the story narrated in *Mahabharata*, when Ganga descended on Earth at Bhagiratha's request, she was borne by Shiva in his locks and released in the form of seven gentle streams. Out of the two streams, Bhagirathi and Alaknanda, which comes together to form Ganga, the modern establishment considers river Bhagirathi to be the original stream of Ganga. However, for the ancients, river Alaknanda was the original stream which united with different tributaries to form the majestic river that descended into plains as Ganga. In *Mahabharata*, Badrinath is always referred to as located on the banks of Ganga which is today called Alakananda."[11] Interestingly, Alaknanda assumes her name only after merging with her tributary Dhauliganga at

Vishnuprayag. Before the confluence, she is known as Vishnu Ganga. Geographically her headwaters originate from the Satopanth glacier nestled deep in the ranges behind Badrinath, but the local priests trace her real origins from Vishnupad, literally meaning foot of Vishnu and philosophically the 'Highest heaven of Vishnu' hence, the river is also called Vishnupadi.[12] The story of Ganga's descent from heaven is widely known among masses, but few are aware of the story of her origins, which is narrated in the Bhagavata Purana.[13]

The story starts as follows: During the eternal cosmic struggle between the Devas and the Asuras, an Asura king Bali decided to conduct a *yajna* (sacrifice) to gain powers. Fearing that Asuras will become invincible, Devas approached Vishnu for help who assured them and took the avatar as a dwarf Brahmin named Vamana. He attended the sacrifice of Bali and when time came for the king to give *dakshina* (gift) to the assembled Brahmins, Vamana asked for land equivalent to his three steps. Bali gave his word to grant the dwarf that much land. Vamana assumed a cosmic form and in his first step he covered all heaven. His toe pierced the vault of heaven and reached Brahmaloka. Out of reverence, Lord Brahma poured water from his sacred *Kamandala* (water pot) to wash the toe of Vishnu. The water after touching the feet of Vishnu became sanctified and flowed across the sky first as *Akash Ganga* (the Milky Way), then, it was redirected by the Pole Star and finally descended in heaven to flow there as the celestial river Ganga. Aeons later, Bhagiratha brought Ganga on Earth to liberate his ancestors.

The celestial river which had descended from heaven to Earth was believed to act as a spiritual ladder that takes souls from their miserable earthly existence to the blissful heaven above. Hence, when time came for Pandavas to depart from the world, they chose to follow the path of Ganga (Alaknanda) to its source.[14] After handing over the kingdom to their grandson Parikshit, Pandavas along with Draupadi, proceeded towards the Himalaya. Visiting the tirthas on the way, they crossed Badrinath and went into the barren wilderness beyond it. Travelling along the banks of Ganga, one by one, the Pandavas fell from exhaustion and died until only Yudhishthira remained. He continued towards his destination, followed by a dog who had been with them since their arrival in the mountains. At last, the divine charioteer of Indra appeared in a golden chariot to escort Yudhishthira to heaven and, after a brief test—where the dog revealed himself to be the god Dharma—Yudhishthira ascended into heaven.

Today, the landscape around Badrinath is marked with places which traces the journey of the Pandavas towards Heaven. Village Mana, located 25 kilometres north of Badrinath, is the last inhabited settlement on the India-China border. Here, over the roaring Saraswati river, is a thick rock serving as bridge between the two shores of the river. Named Bhimpul, it is believed by the locals to be constructed by Bhima who threw a huge rock over the river, so that Draupadi could safely cross to the other side. But Draupadi,

Figure 5 Pandavas on their way to heaven

after travelling a short distance from the bridge, fell down and breathed her last.

Having lost their beloved wife, Pandavas continued their journey with a heavy heart. On their way, they encountered a majestic waterfall, Vasudhara, which, people believe will cease flowing when it sees a sinner. As they ventured ahead, at Laxmi Van, a dense forest of *bhojpatra* (birch) trees, the twins Sahdev and Nakul left for their heavenly abode. After a short distance, Arjun too fell and died in the beautiful meadow of Chakratirtha.

The remaining brothers Bhima and Yudhishthira continued their journey across the rugged terrain, and reached the magnificent Satopanth Lake. Devastated at the

Figure 6 Map showing the route taken by Pandavas on their journey to heaven

death of his siblings, Bhima addressed Yudhishthir, "Brother, our wife is gone. Our brothers are gone. Everything is gone. My life is empty without them. I wish to join them. Why am I not dying?" Yudhishthira calmly replied, "Bhima, until you have your beloved *gada* (mace) with you, you will remain attached to this earthly existence."[15] Hearing this, Bhima threw his mace in the Satopanth Lake and finally attained death. Now, only Yudhishthira remained. He started climbing on to the glacier laden mountain around the lake, the Swargarohini Steps, and finally ascended to the heaven at its summit. Interestingly, the shape of the glacier is such that one of its sides has stair-like structures that are still visible on a clear day.[16]

2

KEDARNATH: ABODE OF SHIVA

> Continuing with his narration on the wonders of north, Garuda said, 'Here in the snowy peaks of the Himalaya resides Maheshwara Shiva. As Purusha, he sports here with Prakriti, the universal goddess. Except for Nara and Narayana, no other being can see him. It was here that the Goddess Uma undertook penance to obtain Shiva as her husband. It was here that Shiva opened his third eye and burned Kamadeva to ashes. It is here that the celestial stream Mandakini and the mountain Mandara can be seen.' [17]

Lord Shiva lived happily with his wife Sati, daughter of Prajapati Daksha. One day, Sati heard that her father was organising a grand sacrifice and all the Gods had been invited. Despite not receiving an invitation from her father and Shiva's opposition to going without one, Sati went to the sacrifice thinking that she was part of the family so did not need an invitation. At her father's place, she was not only made to feel unwelcome, but her family also proceeded to insult her husband. Unable to bear such humiliation, she committed suicide by jumping into the sacrificial fire. When the news reached Shiva, he, in a fit of rage and grief, carried the charred body of Sati and performed the *Tandava* (the dance of destruction). As he carried Sati's body, her body parts fell one by one across the Earth at places which are now known as Shakti Peethas. When nothing remained of her body, Shiva entered a state of severe penance and became wholly disinterested in life

Sati was reborn as Parvati to the king of mountains—the Himalaya and his wife Mena. As she grew up, she realised that her destiny was to reunite with Shiva. But the path of obtaining Shiva as a husband was fraught with difficulties. He was deeply engrossed in meditation and had no intention of becoming a householder again. Taking advantage of Shiva's situation, the demon Tarakasura gained a boon from Brahma that he could die only at the hands of Shiva's son, and started harassing the world.

Powerless against the demon, Gods led by Indra started looking for a solution. Aware of Tarakasura's boon, Shiva's disinterest in worldly affairs and Parvati's identity as the reincarnation of Sati, Indra searched for ways to make the union between Shiva and Parvati possible. He decided to send Parvati to attend to Shiva during his meditation, accompanied by Kamadeva, the god of love, to rouse Shiva. With his powers, Kamadeva caused the advent of spring, full of blooming flowers and chirping birds in the ice-cold Kailash,

Figure 7 An angry Shiva burning Kamadeva

and hit Shiva with his *Kamabana* (the arrow of desire). Shiva awoke and saw a beautiful maiden sitting near him. Under the influence of Kama, amorous desires rose in his heart and he felt a strong attraction towards Parvati. However, Shiva was also quick to realise that what he was feeling was not natural. When he saw Kamadeva hiding in a grove, he understood what had happened. Enraged at Kamadeva's manipulations, Shiva opened his third eye, and instantaneously burned Kamadeva to ashes.

Shiva resumed his meditation leaving Parvati heartbroken. Parvati resolved to win Shiva over on her own and decided to lead a life of atonement in a secluded spot in Himalaya. When Shiva heard about a maiden undertaking such troubles to marry him, he sent the *saptarishis* (seven sages) to observe her. The sages soon returned with their report and confirmed the seriousness of Parvati's efforts. Shiva decided to test her himself and assumed the guise of an ascetic. Carrying his staff and umbrella, he approached the site and was politely welcomed by Parvati. He enquired about her purpose, jeered at her prospects and also ridiculed himself, i.e. Shiva, in many ways, all in an effort to dissuade her. But Parvati stood resolute. Turning away, she asked him to leave as she could not hear another word of insult about Shiva. Pleased, Shiva appeared in his original form and asked her to be his wife. Overjoyed, Parvati accepted and they married in a grand affair attended by all heavenly beings.

Today, the sacred landscape surrounding Kedarnath is marked by the sites where the cosmic events leading to Shiva and Parvati's marriage had taken place. The pilgrims on their way to Kedarnath start their sixteen kilometres long trek from Gaurikund. They bathe in a sacred hot spring which is believed to be the spot where Parvati had performed her penance to win over Shiva as her husband. At a short distance from Gaurikund stands the Triyuginarayan temple, housing the eternal flame around which the cosmic couple took their vows.

Figure 8 Route to Kedarnath along with locations of Panch-Kedar

GAURIKUND AND THE NATHA ORDER

Gaurikund is of special significance for Shaiva ascetics belonging to the Natha order, founded by Matseyndranatha and his disciple, Gorakhnatha in the early mediaeval period. It became particularly influential in Garhwal during sixteenth century, having been patronised by the Panwar kings of Garhwal. One among many sects who worship Shiva-Shakti through tantric rituals, they differ from others in one important way. Rather than following extreme transgressive practices of living in cremation grounds, drinking from skull bowls, etc., which are followed by sects such as Pashupatas and Kapalikas, the Natha order stresses on the power of internal visualisations and meditation. Like other tantric beliefs, they also believe in the transformative power of sexual fluids. At Gaurikund, they consider this transformative power generated by union of Shiva and Parvati to be particularly accessible. Natha yogis harness this power to transform their subtle spiritual body through yogic practices.

The arduous trek which begins from Gaurikund takes the pilgrims through the narrow mountainous valley carved by the river Mandakini. Slowly, as altitude is gained, trees start vanishing from the view while snow began making an appearance, sticking to the rocky walls and edges of the boulder strewn path, melting only for a brief period in the

Figure 9 Kedarnath temple thronged by devotees

monsoon months. After travelling for sixteen kilometres, the narrow path suddenly opens into a wide valley surrounded on three sides by the towering mountains. At the edge of the valley floor, stands the temple of Kedarnath, with Chorabari glacier—the source of river Mandakini, serving as a mesmerising backdrop.

Built from large blocks of greyish stones in vernacular architecture, the temple is accessed through a short flight of steps. At the entrance, one finds the image of Nandi (the guard and vehicle of Shiva) gazing intently at his lord present in the sanctum. Inside, the temple is divided into two sections: the *mandapa* (a pillared hall or pavilion used for public gatherings in a temple) for accommodation of devotees and the *garbhagriha* (the innermost sacred chamber of a temple where the main deity's idol or image is enshrined) housing a rocky outcrop which is worshipped by the devotees as a *jyotirlinga*. A *linga,* an iconic representation of Shiva, is a very common object of worship among people, but jyotirlingas are significant as they are the places where Shiva himself manifested as a fiery pillar of light for the benefit of mankind. The central scripture of Shaivism, Shiva Purana, mentions the names and locations of twelve jyotirlingas spread across the subcontinent. Kedara, on the banks of Mandakini, is one such jyotirlinga.

The Purana says that Sage Nara and Narayana performed penance to propitiate Shiva for a long time.[18] Pleased with their worship, Shiva asked them for a boon. The sages requested him to be eternally present at this spot in the Himalaya for the benefit of mankind. Agreeing to their request, Shiva manifested himself in the form of a jyotirlinga at the spot located on the banks of Mandakini, where today stands the Kedarnath temple. The sight and worship of Shiva in this sanctified region was believed to wash away all the sins of devotees. It was in their desire to expiate themselves of sins committed during *Mahabharata* war that the victorious Pandavas visited Kedarnath to seek the darshan of Shiva. However, the sins they committed during war were not trivial. To win back their kingdom, the Pandavas were forced to kill their cousins – Kauravas and their respected elders – Bhishma and Drona. Shiva, aware of their search but anguished at

Figure 10 Shiva in the form of a bull spotted by the Pandavas

their conduct in the war, went into hiding by assuming the form of a bull. The running bull caught the eye of Pandavas, who realised that this bull was not ordinary. Bhima went after the bull, and caught its hump, but the bull disappeared in the ground; and Pandavas were left with only his hump. Remaining invisible, Shiva asked them to worship the hump to absolve them of their sins. Thus, the hump, in the form of the irregular rock, is how Shiva physically manifested himself in Kedara and which today forms the object of devotion of thousands of pilgrims.

It is believed that when the bull went underground, its body parts reappeared at four other places, apart from Kedarnath. The arms of the bull appeared at Tungnath, face at Rudranath, belly at Madhyamaheshwar, and its head at Kalpeshwar. Together with Kedarnath, they are collectively called the Panch-Kedar and form an important pilgrimage circuit. All these temples are located at considerable heights – above 3000 metres – among the pristine alpine meadows called Bugyals (Refer to Chapter-10). Perched atop a mountain at a height of 3800 metres, Tungnath is the highest Shiva temple in the world. The way to the temple goes through one of the most beautiful meadows of Chopta which comes to life with blooming rhododendrons during spring. All temples except Kalpeshwar become inaccessible during winters when thick snow blankets the landscape.

The period between fifth to sixth century CE in the Indian subcontinent came to be known as the 'Shaiva Age' because it witnessed the rapid rise of many ascetic orders centred around the worship of Shiva. In the initial years, orders like Pashupatas and Kalamukhas following Atimargi or the extreme path of Shiva worship gained influence. They devoted themselves to performing extreme activities like drinking from skull-cups, smearing themselves with ashes, and living in cremation grounds to constantly remind themselves of the temporariness of this world. Other sects rejected the extreme and anti-social character of Atimargi and followed a more sophisticated path, called Mantra Marga or Path of Mantras. They developed a conceptual framework called Shaiva Siddhanta to present a coherent way of worshipping Shiva. The Mantramargi played a more proactive role in public life as founders and administrators of temples and monasteries, and as religious teachers of royal elites.

During Shaiva age, the worship of Shiva as the supreme deity spread rapidly across the subcontinent. From Ellora in the west to Bhubhaneshwar in the east, and Jageshwar in the north to Tanjore in the south, massive temples dedicated to Shiva were constructed by the rulers under the guidance of Shaiva Gurus. Paralleling the construction of temples was the process of compilation and writing down of key scriptures of Shiva Purana and Skanda Purana. These Puranas, encyclopaedic in nature, listed down the important pilgrimage centres connected with stories of Shiva. It is here we find descriptions extolling the religious merits of visiting and performing the essential rituals at Kedarnath, one of the twelve jyotirlingas. Skanda Purana, has a separate section titled Kedar Khanda which not only contains a detailed description of holy sites of Garhwal Himalaya, but also popular stories revolving around marriage of Shiva and Parvati and the birth of their son Kartikeya. Supported by these developments, Kedarnath became a tirtha between the tenth to thirteenth centuries, attracting royal patronage and inclusion in a growing network of pilgrimage circuits.

Kedarnath also finds mention in few recensions of the *Mahabharata*. As per one recension the Pandavas halted for a brief time at Kedarnath before proceeding towards heaven.[19] They bathed in the sacred waters of the Mandakini and prayed to Shiva and their ancestors. They drank the river's pure water and went towards the place of eternal snow to leave their mortal bodies behind. The Skanda Purana describes Kedarnath in a similar manner as the *Mahabharata*. It emphasises the holiness of river Mandakini, describing it as one of the streams of the Ganga that Shiva released from his matted hair. Virtuous people who drink this holy water are released from earthly existence and attain the status of *Ganas* (Shiva's attendants).

Adi Shankaracharya chose Kedarnath as his final resting place, adding to its importance as a tirtha where one achieves liberation. From Badrinath, Shankaracharya made an arduous journey alone on foot to Kedarnath, having instructed his disciples to stay behind in Badrinath. Once he reached the beautiful valley of Kedara, he started his preparations for finally leaving the mortal world. He laid down the staff that he always carried at a spot called Dandi sthal. Then, on a small platform on the banks of Mandakini, he meditated and installed a *sphatika lingam* (a symbol of Shiva made of quartz stone); and, finally, far up in the snow, in one of the caves, he attained *samadhi* (a state of intense concentration) at the age of thirty-two. The Dandi sthal and the sphatika lingam which had served as markers for the presence of Shankaracharya, were washed away by the devastating floods of 2013.[20] The legacy of Shankaracharya was re-established when Prime Minister Narendra Modi unveiled and consecrated the 12 feet-high *murti* (statue) of Shankaracharya in November 2021. Sculpted from black chlorite stone, it depicted Shankaracharya in teaching posture and was purported to be installed at the seer's samadhi sthal which had suffered damage during the floods.

WINTER SEAT

During closing of gates ceremony in winters, a silver *mukhalinga* (linga with Shiva's face) is carried as a representation of Shiva from Kedarnath to Omkareshwar temple at Ukhimath village. Located thirty-seven kilometres downstream, the temple complex at Ukhimath is richly painted with characteristic Pahadi colours of red, blue, and yellow. Apart from being the winter seat of Lord Kedar, the temple houses images of the five Panch-Kedar manifestations of Shiva – Lord Tungnath, Rudranth, Madhyameshwar and Kalpeshwar. The temple walls also contain ancient sculptures highlighting its antiquity.

In 1880, a beautiful princess from the small kingdom of Guler (in Himachal Pradesh) married Pratap Shah, the ruling king of Tehri-Garhwal.[21] A manuscript was handed to her by her mother as part of her dowry. Painted by the royal painter Purkhu, the manuscript was a richly illustrated version of Kedar Kalpa which describes the holy land of Kedarnath, the kingdom of which the princess was going to be the queen. The Kedar Kalpa is classified as a *sthala purana,* a scripture concerned with extolling the sacredness of a particular tirtha of Kedarnath and the numerous benefits accrued by the pilgrims who visit this tirtha. It describes the journey of five *sadhaks* (seekers) of Shiva towards Kedarnath in search of him. On their way, they encounter numerous temptations and dangers, resolve is put to test at each step.

En route to Kedara, these sadhaks bathes in holy streams, climbs steep slopes, walks on rocky paths and cross different cities. These '*puris*'—Indrapuri, Brahmapuri, Nagapuri, Alkapuri—founded by different Gods and celestial beings are always abuzz with celebrations. Within these walled cities, gorgeous and finely adorned damsels play and party together with the ruler of the city who politely greets the sadhaks and enquires their purpose. Each time, the sadhaks give a standard reply; we have come from *mrityu loka* (the mortal world) and are on our way to the abode of Shiva. Hearing their reply, the rulers—through logical arguments and offerings of various luxuries—try to dissuade the sadhaks

Figure 11 The five sadhak bathing in a holy river and praying at the Shiva temple on their way to Kedar

from continuing their journey. But the sadhaks always refuse by saying; if after indulging in the luxuries and desires, they are again condemned to the mortal world from which they seek release, what is the point anyway?

On the way, the group also encounter bloodthirsty tigers and angry guards, but are protected by the power of the *aghora mantra* (a powerful chant of Lord Shiva) which they keep reciting to keep dangers at bay. They meet old men who try to instil doubt in their minds about the existence of Shiva and repeatedly ask them to turn away, but unfazed they carry on. With each successive hurdle, the sadhaks find their bodies becoming beautiful and as strong as a *vajra* (diamond), capable of withstanding everything from blustery cold weather to sharp thorns. They find themselves suddenly remembering the holy Vedas and are able to recite their verses with ease, all by the grace of Shiva. Finally, they reach Kedarnath and are greeted by Shiva and Parvati, who advise them to first visit the abode of the other Gods to see if they would prefer any of them. After visiting all of them, the sadhaks return to Kedarnath and declare that their home is nowhere but at the feet of Shiva. They are granted their request and reside happily in Kedarnath, released from mortal coils to experience eternal bliss with their Lord.

3

GANGOTRI: DESCENT OF GANGA

> Continuing with his narration on the wonders of north, Garuda said, 'Many Siddhas, with their senses always under control, can be seen meditating. The illustrious and truth speaking Munis who have accumulated mystical powers owing to their austerities guard the source of the Ganga. No one can pass beyond this point. Those who try, meet their end.'[22]

In the illustrious Suryavanshi Dynasty[23] of ancient India, there lived a brave king named Sagara. He had two wives, still the king was childless. Together with his wives, he performed great austerity and by the grace of Shiva, both of his queens became pregnant. One gave birth to a son called Asamanjas and the other to a gourd. A divine voice directed King Sagara to take the seeds of the gourd and place them in vessels of ghee. The king complied and thus were born his sixty thousand sons.

His eldest son, Asamanjas, grew up to be a cruel person. He drew much pleasure from throwing helpless children into rivers and see them drowning. After hearing about Asamanjas's wicked deeds, King Sagara exiled him. Asamanjas went away leaving behind his son, Anshuman. A few years later, King Sagara conducted an *ashwamedha yagna* (horse sacrifice) to declare himself the universal ruler of the world. As per the ritual, the horse was left to wander around and was followed by Sagara's sixty thousand sons. Despite the heavy security, the horse suddenly disappeared. The sons went back to the king with the terrible news. In anger, he told them to only return if they found the horse. In their search for the animal, the sons reached the netherworld, where they found the horse roaming freely and sage Kapila meditating nearby. Believing the sage to be the thief, the sons of Sagara hurled abuses at him. Enraged at their lack of respect, Kapila opened his fierce eyes and burned them to ashes.

Sage Narada informed King Sagara about the unfortunate fate of his sons. Grieving, Sagara sent his grandson Anshuman to bring the horse back as the sacrifice could not be left incomplete. Anshuman visited Kapila's hermitage and greeted him with respect. Asking Kapila's permission to take the horse back, he also requested him to tell a way to make his sixty thousand uncles achieve salvation. Pleased by the good manners of the boy, Kapila told him that only Goddess Ganga could save his uncles from their miserable state of existence. Anshuman returned with the horse and the sacrifice was completed. But the salvation of Sangara's sons looked impossible to achieve. For, the celestial river Ganga was not earthbound, but instead, flowed in heaven.

When Anshuman succeeded King Sagara, he tried to bring the Ganga to Earth but failed. His son, Dilip too, met with same result. Finally, it was Dilip's son, Bhagiratha, who successfully executed this difficult task. He journeyed to the Himalaya and lived a life of penance for one thousand celestial years, surviving only on fruits, roots, and water. His intense effort bore fruit and Goddess Ganga appeared before Bhagiratha, ready to grant him a boon. With folded hands, Bhagiratha pleaded with her to descend to Earth and redeem his ancestors by washing over their ashes. Ganga agreed, but warned him of terrible consequences as the Earth will surely shatter from the force of her fall. Except Shiva, no one in the world could bear her force, she explained. Bhagiratha went to Mount Kailash and propitiated Shiva, who agreed to bear the river in his matted locks as she descended from heaven. He stood atop Mount Kailash to catch the turbulent fall of Ganga and then released her in seven gentle streams. Bhagiratha directed the river through the mountains to the place where his ancestor's ashes were kept. As the pure water of Ganga touched them, the souls of Sagara's sixty thousand sons were liberated and became entitled to enter heaven.

The seven streams of Ganga meet at different points on the terrain of Uttarakhand to form a united river which descends from the mountains at Haridwar. The five

Figure 12 Shiva catching Ganga in his locks during her descent at Bhagiratha's request.

confluences of these different streams that form the united river called Ganga are collectively called *Panch Prayag* (five confluences). In Hinduism, *prayag* (the meeting point of two rivers), are considered to be imbued with sacredness and are recommended as a place to perform rituals of prayers, bathing, and ancestor worship. River Alaknanda originates from Satopanth glacier behind Badrinath. Before its confluence, it is known as Vishnu Ganga; and becomes Alaknanda after its merger with Dhauliganga at Vishnuprayag. Nandprayag is the second prayag in the cascading sequence of confluences where Nandakini river joins Alaknanda. The third prayag is Karnaprayag, where Alaknanda merges with

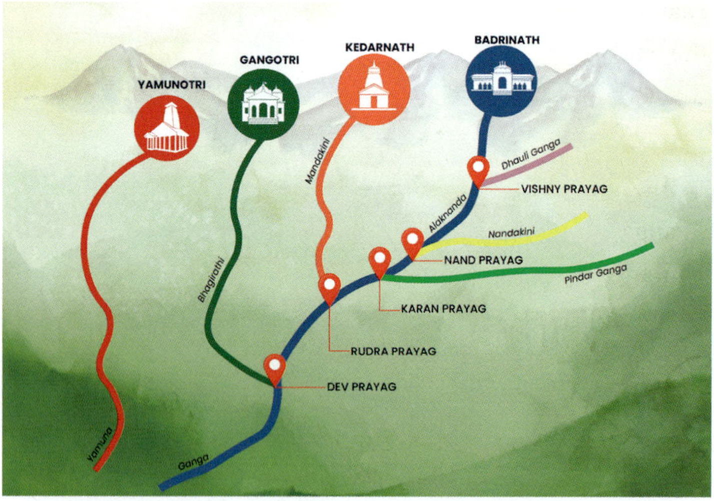

Figure 13 Map showing different streams of Ganga and their confluence

Pindar river whose origins can be traced to the Pindari glacier below the Nanda Devi mountain range. Rudraprayag is the penultimate one, the confluence of the Alaknanda and the Mandakini coming down from Kedarnath. However, out of all the prayags, ritually, the most significant is the fifth—Devaprayag. It is the meeting point of the two principal streams of river Ganga—Bhagirathi (that originates from the Gaumukh glacier in Uttarkashi and flows through Gangotri) and Alaknanda (that originates from the Satopanth glacier in Chamoli). It is from Devprayag that the Ganga river as we know it in the plains, emerges. The one prayag that is not considered a part of the Panch Prayag is Keshav Prayag. It is the confluence of the river Saraswati with Vishnu Ganga/Alaknanda in Mana village just after the latter emerges from the Satopanth lake.

In the *Mahabharata* and other Hindu scriptures, the name 'Ganga' has always been used to refer to river Alaknanda which flows past Badrinath. But today, the other stream Bhagirathi, flowing from the Gaumukh glacier, gets the recognition as Ganga. This shift of perception has its roots in the colonial period. To secure their rule in the newly conquered territories, it was imperative for the British to have an accurate knowledge of the unfamiliar land which they intended to govern. This prompted them to set up institutions dedicated to conducting extensive surveys and mapping of unfamiliar territory using scientific methods.

The first such institution, the Office of the Surveyor General of Bengal, was established by the East India Company in Calcutta in 1767 after gaining control of Bengal in the decisive Battle of Plassey. The first surveyor-general, Major James Rennell, started the process of systematic exploration and mapping of the Ganga basin. He surveyed the Ganga basin lying within the territories of Bengal, Bihar and Odisha that were under British control at the time. Based on his restricted survey, he published a map of the Ganga in 1790 which reiterated the widely held belief among colonial powers that Ganga's source lies in Lake Manasarovar. However, new data collected by the survey proved the map made by Rennell to be incorrect. So, in 1808, Robert Colebrooke, the Surveyor General, decided to send an expedition party to explore the sources of Ganga and its streams. He died soon after, but the work was carried on by an expedition party headed by Lieutenant William Webb, Captain Felix Raper and artist Hyder Hearsay.

The party was dispatched in April 1808 to map and trace the disputed origins of the Ganga. The team's visit to Haridwar coincided with the Kumbh Mela. From there, the team proceeded to Devaprayag where streams of the Bhagirathi and the Alaknanda meet to form Ganga. Instead of following the common route along Alaknanda, a route that had been followed by generations of pilgrims, ascetics and traders, the team decided to follow the Bhagirathi stream to its source. The path along Bhagirathi which had not been travelled much except by locals, proved difficult for the team to navigate. On a precariously narrow path barely wider than a foot, they walked along the shoulder of the mountain with the river gushing six to seven hundred feet below them. They reached Uttarkashi after ten days of continuous travel. It was the last large village on their route, but they prodded on for seven more days and arrived at the village of Bhatwari. Here, they were cautioned by the locals to avoid travelling any further as the road ahead was dangerous. On their way up, the team had noticed that the locals were agile, and could easily cross hurdles which felt unpassable to them. So, such a warning by the locals themselves initially discouraged them from travelling further. But Webb wanted to proceed, so they did, until the terrain ahead—made of steep ascents, imposing rocks, and deep gorges—combined with volatile weather, made it impossible to advance even after leaving their luggage behind. However, the team had gathered sufficient information from the locals about Gangotri—the supposed origin of the river Bhagirathi. Raper writes –

> 'We were now within a six or seven days journey of the place which is called Gangotri and to relinquish it when almost within our reach was very contrary to our inclinations. The pilgrims and the people in the vicinity of this place, who gain their livelihood by bringing

> water from the spot, say that the road beyond Gangotri is passable only for a few miles, when the current is entirely concealed under heaps of snow which no traveller ever has or can surmount.'[24]

The team returned from Bhatwari, and the task of navigating Gangotri was left for years until a soldier decided to undertake the expedition. Born in 1783 in Scotland, James Baillie Fraser journeyed to Calcutta in 1813 to work under the East India Company. His encounter with the Himalaya occurred when he was serving in the company troops, fighting against the Gurkhas who had occupied Garhwal. Although a soldier by occupation, Fraser had a passion for painting and exploration, and the breathtaking landscapes of the Himalaya provided ample opportunity to fulfil both. After the end of war with Gurkhas in 1815, his interest soon turned into tracing the river Ganga and Yamuna to their sources, and along with his brother William, he reached Gangotri in 1815.

> 'We were now in the centre of the stupendous Himalaya, the loftiest and perhaps the most rugged range of mountains in the world. We were at the source of that noble river, equally an object of veneration and a source of fertility, plenty, and opulence to Hindustan; and we had now reached the holiest shrine of Hindu worship which these holy hills contain.' [25]

He left behind a detailed account of the place along with his paintings. He recounts a small stone temple dedicated to Ganga on the bank of river Bhagirathi. It was said to have been constructed by the Gurkha General Amar Singh Thapa a few years before Fraser's expedition, when he had led the invasion in Garhwal. The temple had a small room for priests and was surrounded by caves occupied by pilgrims who came to visit the shrine. The temple was believed to have been the very site where King Bhagiratha had sat meditating which led to the Ganga being brought down from the heavens.

Shortly before Fraser's visit to Gangotri, the region had been won over by Company troops from the Gurkhas. As per the new arrangements, a portion of Garhwal consisting of strategically located Alaknanda valley was to be governed directly by the British. The rest of the region was handed to Sudarshan Shah of Panwar dynasty who was restored back to his ancestral throne sans his royal capital Srinagar in Alaknanda valley, which now became a part of British Garhwal. The king was left to find a new capital for himself, and he selected the site of Tehri, a broad valley drained by Bhagirathi river. Now settled midway between Devaprayag and Gangotri, the dynasty tried to restore its lost fortunes by developing and promoting Gangotri as a pilgrimage centre.

Today, a motorable road runs all the way from the main centres of the state to Gangotri (at 3048 metres), crossing the towns of Uttarkashi and Bhatwari. A town has come up around the temple prompted by an increased pilgrim traffic. Bathing in the ice-cold waters of Bhagirathi, the devotees make their way to the temple on its bank. Enclosed in a spacious courtyard is the white marble shrine, its architecture reflecting influences from Rajasthan. The temple was renovated by Sawai Madho Singh II of Jaipur in the 1930s after it got damaged in an earthquake. Inside the *garbha-griha* (inner sanctum) is the golden image of Goddess Ganga, holding a water pot and lotus and standing atop her *vahana* (vehicle) – *Makara*. She is surrounded by images of her sisters

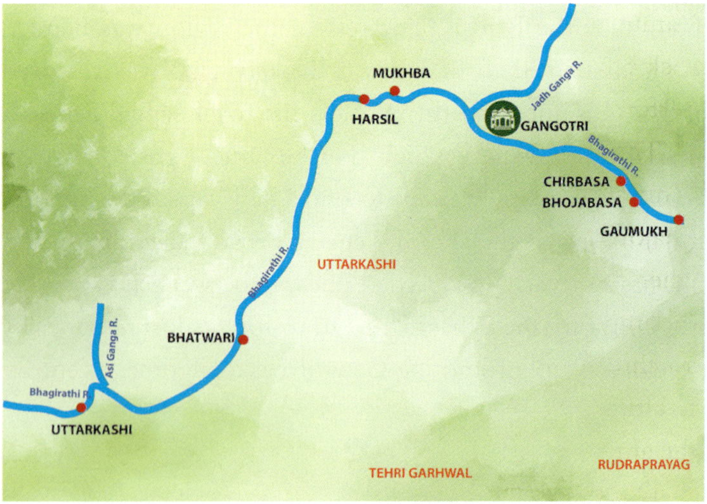

Figure 14 Route to Gangotri and Gaumukh

Figure 15 Gangotri temple

Yamuna, Durga and Annapurna. Outside the temple is a rock called Bhagiratha shila, on top of which Bhagiratha had performed his penance to bring Ganga to Earth.

The main rituals of Gangotri temple are performed by Semwal Brahims hailing from Mukhba village. Ganga *Aarti* (major way of worshipping), is performed in the evening when the Bhagirathi glows under the reflection of hundreds of lamps arranged in multi-tiered structures, and rotated in synchronisation by temple attendants. The chanting of Ganga Lahiri, written by the sixteenth century poet Jagannatha, fills the atmosphere with devotion.

During winters, when the temple is closed, the image of Ganga is brought down to Mukhba, her residence for the next six months. The event occurs on the eve of Bhaiya Dooj festival, and is celebrated as Goddess Ganga coming to stay with her brother Someshwar, the local deity of Mukhba. The gates of Gangotri open on the day of Akshaya Tritiya (in early May) the following year, during the *paath* (chanting and reading) of Ganga Lahiri, Ganga Sahastranam and performance of Ganga Aarti.

Many pilgrims which visit Gangotri are content to have darshan of the river and return after offering their prayers in the temple. But a small subset of travellers, comprising householder devotees, scantily clad ascetics and adventure-seeking trekkers, make it a point to travel further to Gaumukh (4023 metre), the glacial cave from which the celestial Bhagirathi springs forth. The eighteen-kilometre-long trek to Gaumukh starts from the Gangotri temple. From the courtyard wall, a short staircase leads to a gate labelled 'Gangotri National Park.' The dirt trail to Gaumukh is sandwiched between the steep mountain wall and the fast-flowing waters of Bhagirathi. The path passes through Chirawasa and Bhojawasa, where in the recent past, forests of deodar and birch bark were found aplenty. But the region became devoid of vegetation under the pressure of increasing demand for wood in the town.

As one ventures further, the path becomes obstructed with large rocks and boulders. The colours of nature turn to cool shades of grey, brown, and white, and silence blankets the atmosphere, broken only by the distant roaring of Bhagirathi. The gruelling trek ends at Gaumukh, where the glacier hidden under many layers of dirt and sand, forms a cave, and the river Bhagirathi, formed by the melting of snow inside, exits the cave at great speed. Although called the 'cow's mouth', the shape of the cave bears little resemblance to it. Gaumukh is the snout or lowest end of Gangotri glacier, which, measuring 30 kilometres in length and 4 kilometres in width, is the second largest glacier of India after Siachen.

4

YAMUNOTRI: DAUGHTER OF THE SUN

After spending four years at Badrikashram awaiting Arjuna's return from Indraloka, the Pandavas were extremely delighted when he returned with the requisite knowledge of celestial weapons. Then, the Pandavas decided to move on, so they bid adieu to all the sages of the Badrika hermitage. From there, they travelled to the upper reaches of Yamuna river and lived in the vicinity of Mount Yamunotri, whose slopes were covered with snow and were full of hot springs. At the foot of the mountain was a dense forest occupied by many kinds of animals. One day, Bhima went hunting in the forest brimming with majestic deodar trees, tender with touch of snow. The streams hosted thousands of geese and ducks, their quacks echoing in the forest. Bhima felt enthralled by the beauty of his surroundings. His eyes fell on the entrance to a cave, and he decided to explore it. Suddenly, he found himself in the grasp of a gigantic python. The snake revealed himself to be Nahusha, an ancestor of the Pandavas, who was turned into a python due to a curse. Yudhishthira came

Figure 16 Bhima captured by python Nahusha while Yudhishthira requests for his brother's release

to Bhima's rescue. With brother's life at stake, Yudhishthira engaged in a philosophical battle of questions and answers with the python. Yudhishthira's intelligent answers won Nahusha over, and he released Bhima from his painful grasp. Upon freeing Bhima, he himself got liberated from his curse.

Yamunotri is a small picturesque hamlet located at the height of 3291 metres at the foot of Kalind mountain of the Greater Himalayan range of Bandarpoonch. The range, literally named 'Monkey's tail', is where Lord Hanuman extinguished the fire on his tail set by Ravana on Hanuman's journey to Lanka. Although Yamunotri is where people believe Yamuna originates, the actual source lies at a steep distance from the temple, at the height of 4421 metres. The mountain Kalind is aptly named after Surya (Sun), the father of Yamuna, as it hosts the Champasar glacier which melts to give birth to the river. Surrounded by steep slopes, the glacier is very difficult to access and even today, professional trekkers are advised not to go there.

James Baillie Fraser, the Scottish soldier who had first reached Gangotri in 1815, undertook another expedition in the Greater Himalaya in 1820 with the aim to locate the source of 'Jumna'. He left a vivid account of his travels in a journal titled *Journal of a Tour Through Part of the Snowy Range of the Himalaya Mountains, and to the Sources of the Rivers Jumna and Ganges*. Despite guided by local brahmins, navigating Yamuna's gorge proved to be a terrifying experience for Fraser. The trail was practically non-existent and full of loose stones, making it difficult to find a secure footing. A single wrong step meant certain death. Ascending the mountains slowly, the party reached a thick forest with dense undergrowth of creepers and dwarf bamboos which added to their struggles. At many places they found their path blocked by jutting sides of the wall, and had to cross and recross Yamuna from one bank to another several times. The water that had been ice minutes ago pierced their bodies down to their bones. Numbed by the cold and crawling on their hands and knees, they reached a basin slightly wider than the narrow gorge they had traversed. Snow covered mountains, high and impenetrable, rose from the floor of the basin, making any further progress impossible. Three streams formed by melting of the snow, tumbled down the slopes of these mountains towards the basin to form Yamuna. They had, at last, reached their destination, Yamunotri—the source of Yamuna.

Today, the path to Yamunotri starts from the town of Barkot where highways, coming from all other parts of the state, meet. While travelling further, a pilgrim halts at Jamuna Chatti for snacks, Hanumanchatti to view the confluence of Hanuman Ganga with Yamuna, and sees a sign board displaying directions to Phul Chatti. One would surely notice and be curious to know why names of so many places end with the suffix 'chatti'. The word 'chatti' in local parlance signifies resting places where tired pilgrims, in earlier times, would rest and spent the night. Among the four Dhams, Yamunotri has been the most difficult to access, partly because of relatively underdeveloped facilities compared to other Dhams, and partly due to the difficult terrain. Earlier, when motorable roads weren't built all the way to Janakichatti, the trekking route to Yamunotri had eight to nine chattis at regular intervals, with *dharmshalas* (public inns) serving hot food and acting as night shelters for pilgrims arriving from near and far. Today, improvement in road infrastructure has connected all these chattis with an all-weather road, leading to the replacement of dharmshalas with modern hotels, restaurants, and shops. The road ends at Janakichatti, named after Devi Janaki or Sita, which has a small temple dedicated to her husband Ram on the bank of a hot spring.

A steep climb of 6 kilometres from Janki Chatti brings one to Yamunotri. A temple of modest size painted with bright shades of red-yellow-orange stands in the backdrop of Bandarpoonch range. The lavishly decorated image of Goddess Yamuna made from black marble is enshrined in the sanctum. The temple was built by King Sudarshan Shah of Tehri in 1835. It suffers damage due to landslides and earthquakes frequent in the region and is renovated by the authorities from time to time. The priests belong to the Uniyal sub caste of Brahmins, and they are responsible for supervising and managing daily rituals and preparation of prasad.

The distinctive feature of Yamunotri is the presence of several naturally occurring hot springs, a detail recorded in

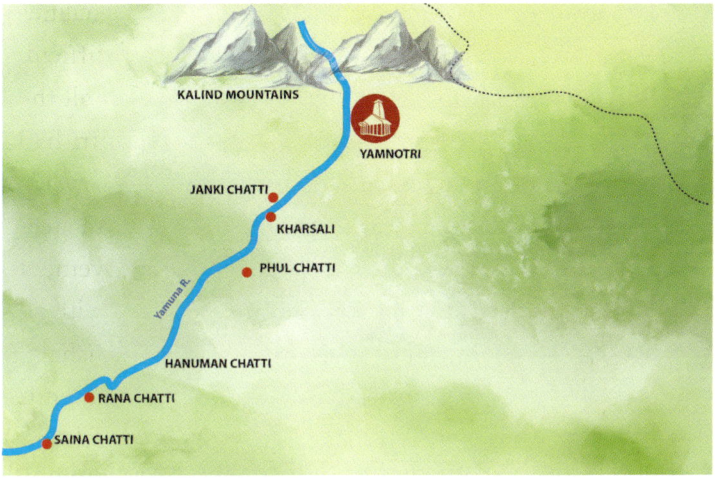

Figure 17 Route to Yamunotri

the *Mahabharata* as well as by James Fraser who visited the region in nineteenth century. Within the temple premises, two hot springs called Surya Kund and Tapta Kund are central to the rituals performed by the pilgrims. Tapta Kund is used by the faithfuls for ritualistic bathing and performing ablutions. Fraser described 'Tapta Kund' as one of the few pools where the cold water of the Yamuna mixed with the hot springs, making the temperature of the pool lukewarm—ideal for bathing. Fraser also bathed in one such pool while a priest chanted prayers and marked Fraser's forehead with sacred mud from the spring. Fraser paid the priest a small fee for his services.

Figure 18 Yamunotri temple

Surya Kund is named after Sun for the temperature of the water measures 88 degree celsius, hence, is unfit for bathing. Fraser describes vapours emanating from the pool and its water being so hot that one could not bear to put their hand in even for a moment. Surya kund has different ritual significance and is used by the pilgrims to prepare prasad. Rice and potatoes sprinkled with salt and tied in muslin cloth are cooked by placing them in the kund's boiling water. The prepared meal is offered before the image of Goddess Yamuna in the temple and after being blessed, is taken home. Like the temple of her sister Ganga at Gangotri, the gates of Yamunotri are closed on the eve of Bhaiya Dooj. Her image is carried to her winter home in Kharsali, a village located near Janaki Chatti. When the time comes to open the gates of all Dhams in early May, Yamunotri opens first.

Yamunotri is a recent addition to the popular list of tirthas as compared to the other three Dhams. The place is not venerated in Puranas or any other scriptures, nor does it find much mention in colonial surveys, gazetteers and travelogues except in the account of James Fraser. The three volume Himalayan gazetteer, compiled in 1885 by Edwin Thomas Atkinson, mentions smallest and farthest located villages of the Garhwal mountains. They contain elaborate descriptions of Kedarnath, Badrinath and Gangotri but Yamunotri is absent in them. The probable reason for its lack of popularity could be the fact that the Yamuna and its tributaries were not considered auspicious and no religious merit was attached in bathing in their waters, while Ganga and its tributaries had always been held as the most sacred. Another factor could be that Jaunsar-Bawar, the region drained by Yamuna, has historically been less populated and economically poor, which meant fewer amenities for pilgrims. However, the status of Yamunotri changed with the shifting of the court of the Panwar kings from Srinagar to Tehri in 1815. The construction of the temple at Yamunotri by the King Sudarshan Shah in 1835 initiated the development of Yamunotri as a tirtha. Slowly, with the steady arrival of pilgrims, it became a part of the Char-Dham circuit.

Coming back to the description of wonderful treasures of north by Garuda says 'It is for these and other incidents (as described in the beginning of previous three chapters) that the northern region is superior to all quarters. And because this region is superior to all, therefore, it is called the north or uttara. This quarter saves you from sins and one can attain salvation here. It is also because of its saving power i.e., Uttarana that it is called Uttara (north).'[26] Thus, the majestic bird ends his narration by declaring the north to be the most superior of all quarters, for they contain the Himalaya, the abode of tirthas, of which Char-Dham are the most holy and venerated today by millions of people.

5

HARIDWAR: THE GATEWAY TOWN

While travelling around the world, the bad-tempered Sage Durvasa saw a beautiful celestial nymph holding a garland of exquisite samaltaka flowers. He obtained the garland from her and gifted it to Indra, the Lord of Indraloka who was, at that moment, accompanied by his retinue of Devas and celestial beings. Indra was sitting atop Airavata, his elephant mount, so he placed the wreath over the elephant's head. Irritated by the fragrance, Airavata threw the garland on the ground. Durvasa became furious at the rejection of his gift. He roared at Indra, "Drunk upon your power, you have become arrogant and did not properly honour my gift. You mistook me for other gentle sages who would forgive your folly, but forgiveness is not in my nature. Hence, I curse you that you along with other Devas will lose that power on account of which you swell with pride."

Swiftly dismounting from Airavata, Indra begged the irascible sage for forgiveness but Durvasa refused to entertain him and went away. Soon, the curse started having its effect on the Devas and they lost their strength. Heaven became lustreless. Taking advantage of this opportunity, the Daityas attacked Indraloka and defeated the Devas. The Gods led by Indra rushed to Lord Vishnu for help. Vishnu suggested that in order to regain their strength, they should negotiate a pact with the Daityas and jointly churn the ocean of milk to obtain Amrit, the drink of immortality.

As directed, the Devas gathered the magical herbs and threw them in the ocean of milk. Using Mount Mandar as a churning rod and the serpent Vasuki as a rope, the great churn began. Devas held the tail of the snake while the Daityas held the side of its head. Suddenly, the mountain began sinking into the ocean. To save this significant task from disruption, Vishnu took the *Kurma Avatar* (a cosmic tortoise) and supported the mountain on his back.

The churning continued and the ocean started yielding valuable treasures from its milky depths. First came Surabhi, the divine cow and fulfiller of all wishes; Ucchasharivas, the divine horse with the speed of wind; Parijata, the celestial tree laden with fragrant flowers; Kaustabha, the foremost of all gems, and Halahala, the most powerful poison of the universe. At last, emerged Dhanvantari, the cosmic physician, clad in white clothes and holding *kumbh* (a golden pot) full of *amrit* (nectar). A fight ensued between Devas and Daityas and the pot was stolen by the Daityas. Before they could drink the nectar, Vishnu saved the day by assuming the form of Mohini, the enchantress, and successfully brought the nectar to the Devas. The strength of the Devas was restored as they consumed the divine potion, and defeated the Daityas

Figure 19 Appearance of Dhanvantri with the pot of Amrit during the churning of ocean

who fled to the netherworld. As the popular version of this story goes, during the tussle between Devas and Daityas over the possession of the elixir, four drops of amrit fell at four different spots on the Earth. These places became infused with a kind of sacred potency and today they are known as Haridwar, Prayagraj, Ujjain and Nashik, the sites to host Kumbh Mela every twelve years.

THE TORTOISE SHELL FOSSIL

In 1834, colonial palaeontologist Hugh Falconer and Proby Cautley, discovered a spectacular and well-preserved field of 2.5 million years old fossils in the shallow depths of Shivaliks on Uttarakhand-Himachal border. Among these fossils, was a gigantic tortoise shell, 12 feet in diameter and 6 feet in height. This was the time, when the colonists had shown an interest in understanding the customs and traditions of the country and, through Asiatic society, were enthusiastically translating the Sanskrit Puranas into European languages. The discovery of the fossil ignited Falconer's imagination and he connected it with the Kurma avatar of Vishnu. He at first named the fossil *Megalochelys sivalensis,* which means 'the mega tortoise from the Shivaliks'. But the name neither conveyed the colossal dimensions of the tortoise of which it was once a part, nor the apparent link to the tale of Kurma avatar. So, the name was changed to *Colossochelys atlas*, which translated to 'the colossal turtle holding the world'.

Haridwar, located on banks of river Ganga, is one of the oldest continuously inhabited settlements of the country and one of the holiest places of Hinduism. Two localities—Gangadwar and Kankhala—finds repeated mentions in *Mahabharata* and various Puranas. Sage Lomasha introduced the place to Pandavas on their way to Badrikashram. He spoke:

> 'O Yudhishthira, the spot where Ganga rushes past, cleaving the foremost of mountains which is frequented by Gandharvas and Yakshas and Rakshasas and Apsaras, is called Gangadwar.'[27]

Gangadwar literally means the Gateway of Ganga. The place is aptly named as it served as the starting point for pilgrims and ascetics on their way to sacred places located far and deep within the formidable chain of Himalaya. In earlier times, Gangadwar and Kankhala were two separate hamlets located at some distance from each other, today they fall within the municipal limits of Haridwar city.

Today, Har-ki-Pauri is considered to mark the precise spot where Ganga lands into the plains after making her way through the mountains. This famous ghat, meaning 'Steps of Shiva', is situated on a crescent moon shaped stream of Ganga which branches out a short distance northwards and merges with the main channel after passing the Ghat. During the evening aarti for mother Ganga, the ghat lightens up when priests spin thousands of lamps in unison while chanting mantras. The place is always alive with a multitude of people from all over India and abroad, some silently praying on the steps leading to the river, others bathing in its cold waters, while many perform the *sanskars* (rites of passage) with the help of *pandits* (the priests).

Sanskars, are a collection of rituals which are mandated to be performed by every pious Hindu at some chosen important stages of his life. Many of these rites, especially the funerary rites, are recommended by the scriptures to be performed at the banks of Ganga for religious merit. Mahabharata explains it as:

> 'Those creatures whose bodies have been sprinkled with the sacred waters of Bhagirathi or whose bones have been laid in the channel of that sacred stream, do not fall away from heaven at any time. Those men who use the waters of Bhagirathi in all their acts, surely ascend to heaven after departing from this world.'[28]

Thus, the tradition of spending one's last days and performing the last rites of the deceased on the banks of Ganga is very old. In the *Mahabharata*, Bhishma, the son of

Goddess Ganga and Shantanu, the patriarch of Kuru family, proceeded to Gangadwara after the death of his father. As he began preparations to perform *shraddha* (ritual ceremony of making offerings to ancestors), Ganga helped him by inviting many illustrious sages residing in vicinity to attend the ceremony. Similarly, after the end of the *Mahabharata* war, King Dhrithrashtra, father of Kauravas, handed the throne to his nephews, the Pandavas, and went to Gangadwar along with his wife Gandhari and sister-in-law Kunti. One day, a fiery fire broke out in the forest surrounding their hamlet and engulfed them.[29] When the news of their death reached Hastinapur, King Yudhishthira, along with his brothers and royal ladies, came to Gangadwar to perform their last rites. Clad in simple clothes, they stood knee deep in Ganga and offered oblations of water to the departed. The King then ordered the Brahmins, well conversant in the scriptures, to perform the proper rites of cremation. On the twelfth day of the ceremony, the King conducted the shraddha ceremony of his deceased relations and donated a large sum in their name. These funerary rituals continue to present day. Hindus from all over the world come to Haridwar to perform final funerary rites of their loved ones and immerse their ashes in river Ganga. Many dharmashalas stand on the ghats, some built centuries ago and some new, catering to the diverse set of pilgrims coming to Haridwar.

THE SHAKTI-PEETHAS OF HARIDWAR

Overlooking Har-ki-Pauri are the temples of two goddesses, Chandi Devi and Manasa Devi, on the summit of two hills of the Shivaliks located on the opposite banks of Ganga. The temple of Chandi Devi is on Neel Parbat while Mansa Devi, Goddess of snakes, resides on the Bilwa mountain. Both act as guardian deities of the city and their temples are thronged by devotees visiting the shrines through cable cars.

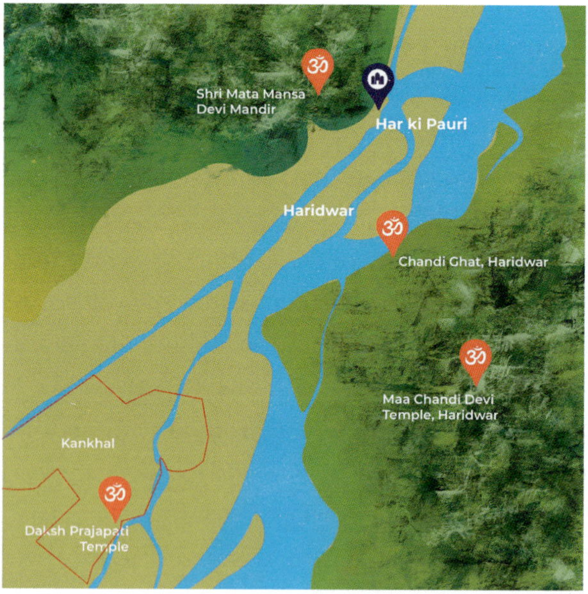

Figure 20 The Shakti-Peethas of Haridwar

Figure 21 Har-ki-Pauri in Haridwar thronged with pilgrims

The epic literature also mentions the holy tirtha of Kankhal located a few kilometres south of Har-ki-Pauri, about which it says that 'Bathing at Kanakhala, and fasting there for three nights, a person reaps the merit of the horse-sacrifice and goes to heaven.'[30] The Dakshesvara temple at Kankhal is dedicated to Prajapati Daksha, son of Brahma and father of Sati. As per Shiva Purana, Daksha had organised a grand sacrifice at Kankhal and invitations were sent to all the Gods except Shiva, his son-in-law, whom Daksha did not like. When Sati attended the sacrifice uninvited, she was hurt and humiliated at the indifference of her family towards her husband and committed suicide by jumping into the sacrificial fire. Hearing of the demise of her beloved wife, Shiva's wrath knew no bounds, and a terrible form called Virbhadra sprang from his anger. Virbhadra destroyed Daksha's sacrifice and cut off his head. At the behest of other Gods, Shiva revived Daksha who then repented and installed a linga near the altar to worship Shiva. The site of Dakshesvara temple is said to mark the place where these events occurred. Sati Kund, where Sati cast off her body by jumping into the fire, is also present within the temple premises.

Apart from the routine visits to its ghats, Haridwar comes alive during the celebration of the Kumbh Mela. Held after every twelve years, and on a rotation basis in one of the following locations— the banks of river Ganga in Haridwar, the confluence of the Ganga and the Yamuna in Prayagraj, the banks of river Godavari in Nasik and river Shipra in Ujjain—the festival is the largest religious congregation of the world. In popular imagination, the celebration of Kumbh is linked with the story of the Churning of Ocean narrated at the start of the chapter. Although the story finds mention in major Puranas and the *Mahabharata*, the particular episode of amrit falling on Earth is not found in any of them. So, what are the true origins of this festival and what connects the places where it is held?

From a careful study of references to 'Kumbh' in Puranas—Skanda Purana, Vishnu Purana, and Narada Purana—it is observed that the word is used in connection with a particular astronomical conjunction.[31] When Jupiter is in the constellation of Aquarius whose sign represents a pitcher full of elixir and the Sun has entered in Aries, the conjunction so formed is called Kumbh. This time period called *Kumbh Parva* was considered highly auspicious. Bathing in the waters

Figure 22 Pilgrims bathing in the Ganga during Kumbh Mela

of Ganga at Haridwar during this time was believed to yield merit greater than one accumulated by thousand sacrifices and not achieved by bathing million times at another period of the year.[32] Hence, in the scriptures, Kumbh was exclusively used with reference to bathing in Ganga when Jupiter and the Sun are in special positions.

While Haridwar and Prayagraj are located on the banks of Ganga, the river Shipra and Godavari are also indirectly associated with Ganga in Puranic literature. For instance, in Brahma Purana, Godavari is called as Gautami Ganga or Ganga of the South. Similarly, in Skanda Purana, it is written that Ganga went to Lord Brahma and complained that she had become too burdened by the sins of those bathing in her waters which has turned blue. Brahma suggested her to go to Mahakaleshwar in Ujjain. As soon as Ganga entered that sacred place, she became white and merged with river Shipra flowing nearby. Henceforth, Shipra was also called *Neel Ganga*. Thus, the connection of four towns with the celebration of Kumbh Mela has very much to do with their connection with Ganga, and her being bestowed with purifying and strength-giving properties like amrit over which the Devas and Daityas had fought.

The organisation of the Mela in each of the four towns is dictated by the position of Jupiter and Sun. The festival originates in Haridwar, where it is conducted during the astronomical period called Kumbh, i.e., when Jupiter is in the Aquarius constellation and Sun is in Aries. The Mela is held at Prayagraj when Jupiter is in the Taurus constellation and Sun in Aries; at Nashik & Ujjain when Jupiter is in Leo and the Sun in Cancer (Nashik) and Aries (Ujjain) respectively. Since the planet Jupiter takes 12 years to complete one revolution around the Sun, *Poorna* (full Kumbh Mela) takes place after twelve years. The festival is attended by people from all over the world who congregate at a makeshift city erected near the rivers. Different *akharas* (religious orders) and their leaders start their preparations and gather in advance at the designated ghats. The core ritual of Kumbh Mela is bathing in waters of Ganga or the river equivalent to Ganga when planets are in favourable positions. The act is believed to release one from the eternal cycle of life and death and helps in attaining *moksha* (liberation). Sadhus from different akharas lead these bathing processions, known as *shahi snan* (royal bath) after which common devotees take the lead. In the beginning, this mega-gathering was held only in Haridwar and included bathing in Ganga as its core ritual. Such is the power of belief that today, river Ganga invisibly connects the four holy towns where the festival is held every four years.

PART B

BEING PAHADI: THE LOCAL CULTURES

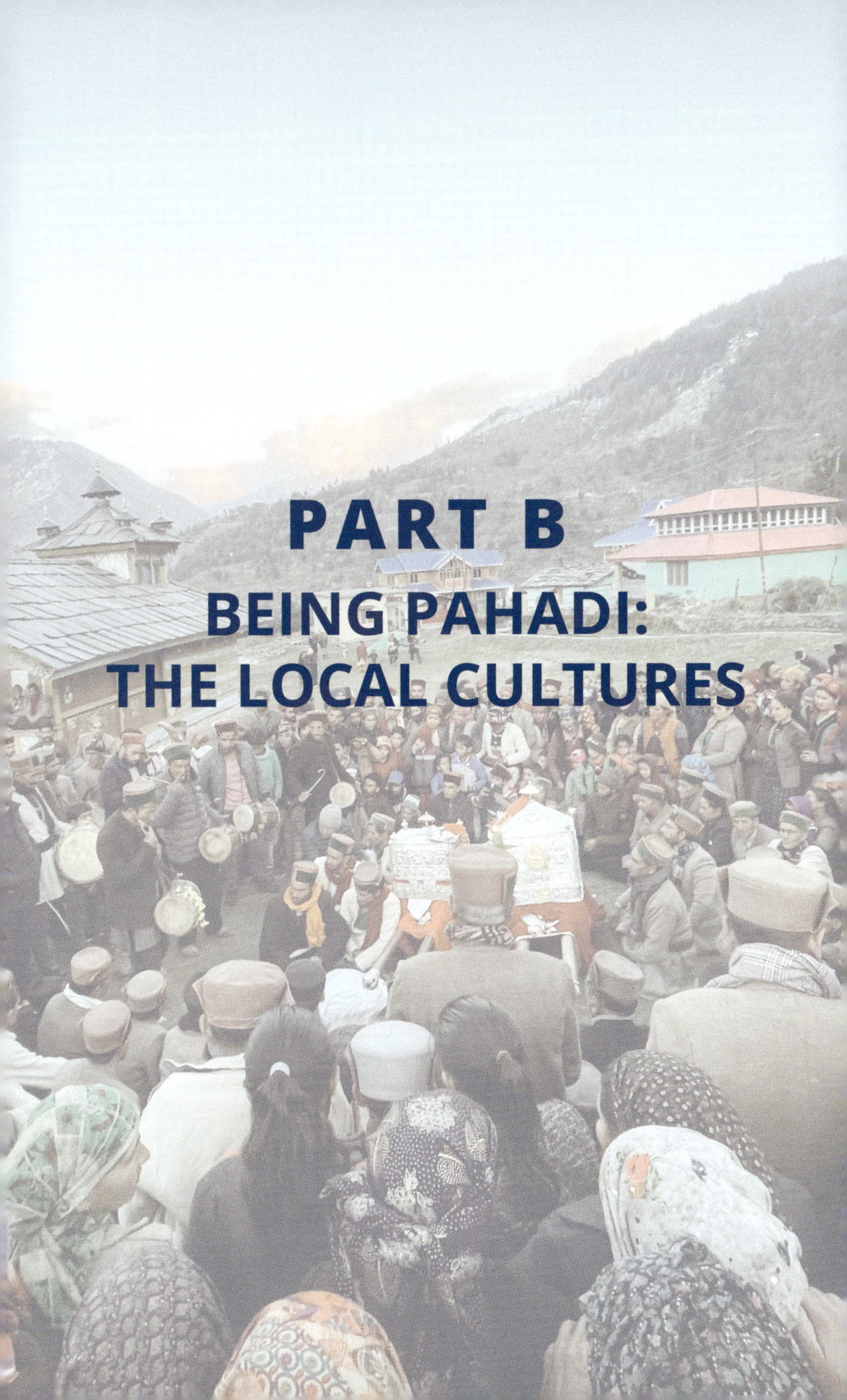

6

NANDA DEVI: THE MOUNTAIN GODDESS

The year was 1942. Exhausted from a steep climb, a party led by forest ranger Hari Kishan Madhwal, came to a stop. Although it was September and winter was yet to come, the place was cold enough to freeze the sweat on Madhwal and the band of porters he was leading. Rain-bearing clouds enveloped them at 4,500 metres, obscuring the view completely. Proceeding any further was dangerous; for one, they were far away from any human habitation; the second and more immediate reason was that they had balanced themselves on a precipitous ridge. One misstep, and they could plunge into the sharp slopes on either side. The region was devoid of vegetation and remained under thick layers of snow for most of the year. It was only for a brief period during the monsoon months of August and September that the ice melted, and one could hope to find in these lands the rare and fresh Brahma Kamal and Phen Kamal which the party was hoping to collect. The clouds suddenly parted and sunlight shone through, giving the expedition a clear view of the area for the first time. Just along the ridge was a small rounded lake embedded in the snow. Its bright green surface shone in the sunlight and, as the eyes of the party adjusted, they froze. Before them lay a ghastly sight.[33]

Surrounding the emerald depression were hundreds of human bones. Some were half-covered in gravelly debris while others protruded from the ice. Some others still had flesh attached to the bones, covered in torn clothes and their faces twisted. Believing that they had arrived in an earthly version of hell, many members of the party became terrified and started retreating. They fled, leaving Madhwal with the responsibility of reporting to his superior, the deputy Commissioner of Garhwal, R.V. Vernede, the horror his party had just encountered. Vernede was equally puzzled and horrified, and so was his reporting officer, Mr. T.G. Acton, the Commissioner of Kumaon. It was the peak of the Second

Figure 23 Skulls at Roopkund

World War, and the British were particularly concerned about Japan, who had been victorious in many battles in Asia and was constantly threatening to invade Britain's prized possession—India. With the imminent threat of Japanese invasion looming in their minds, the British assumed that the skeletons were the remains of Japanese soldiers who had recently died while trying to sneak into India undetected.

The lake, now famous as Skeleton Lake, is Roopkund, a pristine yet mysterious body of water tucked into a remote corner of the Garhwal Himalaya. Located 58 kilometres from Badrinath at an altitude of 4,500 metres and at the foot of Mount Trishul (7,120 metre), it is accessible only by trekking across mountainous slopes and meadows. After Independence, the interest in decoding the identity of the skeletons caught the fancy of many. The Japanese-soldiers theory was discredited but many others took its place. Some believed that the remains belonged to soldiers from the army of a Dogra General, Zorawar Singh, who had invaded Tibet in 1841. The conjecture was that they had lost their way while returning and had died from starvation and cold. Others believed that a group of ascetics, following rigid rituals, committed mass suicides near the lake. When, in the 1960s, carbon dating revealed that the remains dated back to twelfth to fifteenth century, many thought that the army of Delhi Sultan Muhammad bin Tughlaq had perished there. Despite several theories put forward to explain the mystery of the skeletal remains, none of them was sufficiently convincing. A plausible hypothesis emerged once the scholars began paying attention to the folklore of the villages of the surrounding areas, the songs and stories passed down across generations, preserving the memories of the distant past. The songs served as a cautionary tale against what happens when one violates the rules laid by the mountain Goddess Nanda, the Supreme Goddess and the presiding deity of the region.

Folklore recounts how the arrogant King Jasdhawal of Kannauj did not extend proper respect to Nanda when she came to visit his kingdom.[34] Her curse brought numerous misfortunes upon him and, to atone for his sins, the king embarked on a pilgrimage to Devi's holy abode, taking along his pregnant wife and an entourage of dancing girls and musicians. He reached the mountains and was about to proceed further when the locals cautioned him to leave his wife and party behind and carry on alone. Disregarding their warning, the king continued and set up camp in the holy sanctuary. To entertain himself, he made the musicians and courtesans stage a dance performance while his queen went into labour. Furious at the desecration of her sacred abode by the haughty conduct of the king, Nanda turned the dancing courtesans into stones and sent a fierce hailstorm that engulfed the entire group. Everyone perished, and their skeletons remained there to this day, cautioning visitors to maintain proper decorum or invite the goddess's wrath. Whether the people who perished indeed belonged to the conceited king's entourage is difficult to say, but scientific analysis of the skeletal remains has provided some definitive clues.

In 2004, National Geographic assembled a team of scientists and researchers from various disciplines and sent them on an expedition to Roopkund. They studied the area around the lake and found that most remains were remarkably preserved in ice, with the flesh and clothes still intact on some. Professor Subhash Walimbe, an anthropologist, and Professor Joglekar, a bio-archaeologist from Deccan College, Pune, concluded from their analysis that many people had died from sharp blows to their skulls. The injuries indicated that the blows were not from sharp objects, like swords or spears, but from smooth, round objects the size of cricket balls. The most plausible explanation for a scenario where so many people had suffered similar injuries was that something had fallen from the sky.[35] William Sax, an anthropologist from Harvard who was part of the team, recalled that years ago, on his first trek to the lake, he was caught in a sudden blizzard and escaped with his life through sheer luck. He was carried to the nearest village where it took him ten days to recover. In folklore too, Nanda punishes the king and his retinue by sending 'iron-like hail.'

A few tissue and bone samples from the skeletons preserved in the lake were sent to a lab at Oxford University for analysis. More precise dates emerged, clustering around the ninth century. DNA analysis found the presence of two distinct sets of people; one short and broad-faced with grooves on their neck and back made from routinely carrying luggage; the other, tall, and sharp-faced. The presence of ritual objects like bamboo staves helped piece the puzzle together. A plausible hypothesis emerged. In the ninth century, a group of pilgrims arriving from the plains hired the locals as porters. This group was caught in a sudden hailstorm while traversing the narrow ridge overlooking the lake. They perished by sustaining fatal injuries from hailstones, their remains scattered down the ridge and into the lake.[36]

This scientific study of the skeletal remains also revealed the antiquity of pilgrimage which operated on this route. This pilgrimage called Raj Jat is dedicated to Goddess Nanda and forms one of the world's longest and most challenging journeys. This pilgrimage is a testimony to how nature, kinship, geography and mythology are closely intertwined in the culture of *Pahad.* To understand the spectacular journey of faith, it is better to first understand the natural landscape and the cultural meanings associated with it.

The Holy Sanctuary of Nanda Devi

Goddess Nanda, a manifestation of *shakti* (cosmic energy), is considered an incarnation of Parvati, the daughter of the Himalaya and consort of Lord Shiva. Equally venerated in Garhwal and Kumaon, Nanda is inevitably associated with the Himalayan landscape. Uttarakhand's tallest mountain

Figure 24 View of Mount Nanda Devi

is revered as the embodiment of the goddess and is named after her. Measured by British surveyors in 1820 to be 7,816 metres tall, it remained India's highest mountain, until the discovery of Mount Kanchenjunga in 1847.[37] The mountain, composed of the twin peaks of Nanda Devi and Nanda East, is enclosed by a continuous ring of lofty mountains, making it inaccessible to the world outside.

Beginning in the 1800s, several attempts were made by mountaineers, army officers and administrators to breach this formidable barrier. Starting from George William Traill in 1830, the second Commissioner of Kumaon; mountaineer Tom Longstaff in 1905; Hugh Ruttledge in 1925; all these attempts were made to enter the sanctuary from the east along the Pindari and Milam glaciers. In 1830,

Traill reached a pass linking Nanda Kot and Nanda Devi, but was unable to cross it. It was later named as 'Traill's Pass' in his memory. Colonel Tom Longstaff, along with two Swiss guides, managed to climb a col (the lowest point on the ridge connecting two peaks) of Nanda Devi East, a short distance from its summit. They became the first party to gain a rare and distant view inside the sanctuary. However, since the descent was very dangerous, they could not enter inside the sanctuary. The point of his ascent was named 'Longstaff's Col' in his memory.

Hugh Ruttledge, a mountaineer, and former deputy Commissioner of Almora crossed the Traill's Pass successfully but was unable to proceed any further. His three unsuccessful attempts to reach inside the sanctuary prompted him to write a letter[38] to the *London Times* saying that 'Nanda Devi imposes on her votaries an admission test as yet beyond their skill and endurance' and entering the sanctuary was more difficult than accessing the North Pole. He further elaborates on the insurmountable challenge posed by the topography of the place. 'A seventy-mile barrier ring on which stand twelve peaks of over 21,000 feet which has no depression lower than 17,000 feet, except in the west, where the river Rishi Ganga, rising at the foot of Nanda Devi, has earned for itself what must be one of the most terrific gorges in the world.'

The break in this long chain of unsuccessful attempts came when two mountaineers, Eric Shipton and Bill Tilman, spurred by Ruttledge's article set their minds to breach the

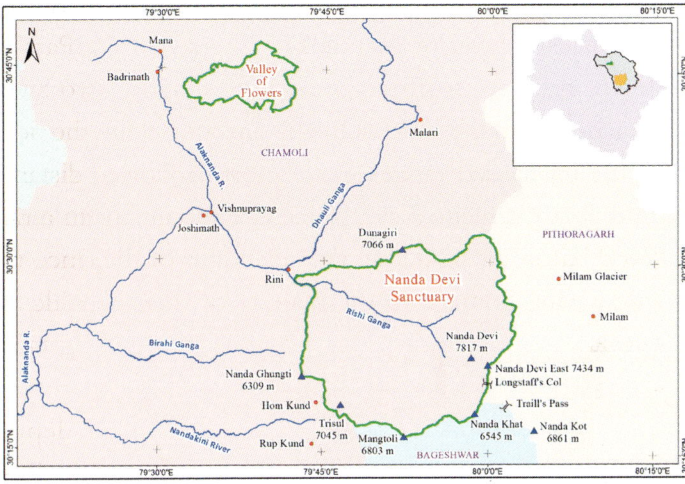

Figure 25 Map showing the major peaks of Nanda Devi sanctuary

sanctuary. Instead of attempting to enter the sanctuary from the east like their predecessors, they decided to focus their efforts on the west. The only opening from the west was the highly dangerous gorge made by Rishi Ganga river coming from inside the sanctuary. In 1934, making their way through the narrow and menacing gorge, with their lives hanging by a thread, Shipton and Tilman became the first people to set foot inside the sacred sanctuary of Nanda Devi.[39] The experience of navigating the most impossible of the mountain barrier was described by Shipton as,

> 'Towards sunset the rain cleared off and, as we sat round our juniper fire, we witnessed a heavenly

unveiling of the great peaks of the basin. First appeared the majestic head of Nanda Devi herself, frowning down upon us from an incredible height, utterly detached from the Earth. One by one, the white giants of the un-named ranges to the north followed suit; until at last it seemed as if the entire mountain realm stood before us bathed in the splendour of the dying sun, paying homage to the majesty of their peerless queen.'[40]

The ring of mountains forming the sanctuary around Mount Nanda Devi are mostly named after Goddess Nanda. They include Nanda Khat (Nanda's bed), Nanda Kot (Nanda's Fort) and Nanda Ghunti (Nanda's veil). Although Mount Nanda Devi is revered by locals as the physical manifestation of the goddess, her residence is believed to be at Mount Trishul, locally known as Kailash, where she lives with her husband Lord Shiva. Slightly smaller than Mount Nanda measuring 7,120 metres, Mount Trishul is a part of mountain barrier and stands in front of Mount Nanda when viewed from the west. At the base of Trishul is the little glacial lake of Homkund, which is the terminating point of the Raj Jat pilgrimage. After having understood the geography of the region, the next thing to know is the story of Nanda Devi which provides the context and meaning to the Raj Jat.

The story begins in the fertile valley of Rishau, where once lived an old Pahadi couple, Hemant and Mainuli. They were childless so they prayed for an offspring. Goddess Nanda heard their prayers, and a beautiful girl was born to them. The child shone with divine radiance and was named Nanda, as she brought joy (*ananda*) to everyone. Soon, Nanda grew up, and her parents began to look for a suitable groom for her. Meanwhile, in Devaloka, Shiva was engaged in deep meditation. Other Gods became apprehensive that he would become too powerful and requested Rishi Narada to distract Bhole Shankar. Narada set off for Kailash and, once there, refused to accept the hospitality offered by Shankar. Shaking his head, he said to him, "I cannot accept anything from you. You are not a proper householder because you do not have a wife." Shankar, puzzled, asked what Narada wanted. This was the opportunity Narada had been waiting for. He continued, "I have found a suitable match for you. The girl is the most beautiful I have ever seen and is capable in every way of becoming your mate." Now, Shiva was intrigued. Narada filled him in with more details and, gaining Bhole's permission, went to Rishau, seeking Nanda's hand for the God. Hemant and Mainuli accepted the marriage proposal and a wedding date was set

The marriage took place as per customs, and soon, it was time for the bride to leave her parents. The whole village gathered to see Nanda off. Teary-eyed, Nanda bid her parents and home goodbye. The newlyweds' journey to Kailash was

Figure 26 Creation of Roopkund by Shiva

long with multiple stops along the way. Wherever Nanda halted, people warmly welcomed her. But she was most pleased by the hospitality offered in the village of Nauti. The place reminded her of her home in Rishau. She appointed the Nautiyals to be her priests and, henceforth, to take care of travel arrangements whenever she returned home. Together, Shiva and Nanda climbed up to Kailash. Human settlements were soon replaced by emerald green meadows stretching as far as the eyes could see. At one point, Nanda became tired and thirsty, but no water body was in sight. Shankar pierced the ground with his trident, and a spring burst out. A pool quickly formed at that spot. As Nanda bent to get a drink, she halted to stare at her reflection. She looked breathtaking in her bridal attire. As she sat admiring her beauty, Shiva stared at her, mesmerised. He named the pool Roopkund—the pool of beauty in her honour. They continued their journey and reached Kailash.

With the passage of time, Nanda began to feel unhappy and restless in Kailash. Her new home was a stark contrast to her natal home. On the one hand, the valley of Rishau was green and full of warmth and the laughter of people. Flowers bloomed bright and birds chirped from the long, hanging branches of oak trees. Kailash, on the other hand, was devoid of any such warmth. There was snow for as far as the eye could see. Their house was barely furnished and had no luxuries. Her bed was made of hard ice, her clothes of bark and rough wool. There was nothing to eat except roots and fruits. There was no one to keep her company but her husband who was too occupied with his meditation to pay her any attention. Nanda grew angry at her parents and elders of Rishau for selecting such an unsuitable match for her. Gradually, her anger started to have an unexpected effect. Rishau was soon engulfed in various misfortunes. Concerned, its twelve elder sages consulted an astrologer from Banaras, who told them about Nanda's situation and advised Hemant and Mainuli to host a pooja and invite Nanda to attend it. Two bumble bees were created by the sages and an invitation to Nanda was transcribed on their wings. They flew to Kailash with their missive. Upon receiving it, Nanda's happiness knew no bounds. The prospect of going back to her mait and meeting her parents and friends was delightful. She asked Shiva for his permission to go. He reluctantly gave in but with one condition: she was to come back to Kailash before the rains stopped and the snow started setting in. Nanda agreed.

Nanda received a grand welcome in Rishau. Her parents hugged her and fed her the choicest delicacies. The villagers showered her with fine clothes, jewellery and other offerings. Nanda wholeheartedly enjoyed her stay in the village, reliving many fond memories of her childhood. But soon, it was time to return to Kailash. The joy ended and melancholy descended upon the people of Rishau. A palanquin, carved from mango wood and topped with bamboo parasols, was prepared for Nanda. With tears in her eyes, Nanda bade farewell to her

Figure 27 Nanda's journey to her sauras at Kailash

parents and her Rishau. The villagers accompanied her on her journey back and, as the procession progressed, everyone started joining it. Her brothers, and the local Gods Danu and Latu also arrived to escort her. Finally, the entourage reached the base of Kailash, from where the goddess had to start her journey alone. Nanda blessed everyone present and bade them adieu until the next time of her journey.

Nanda Devi has been closely worshipped by the successive dynasties of Garhwal and Kumaon. The cult of the royal goddess is pan-Indian, where kings usually adopt a goddess as their *Kul-Devi*, or patron goddess, who is believed to be the factor behind their military success and prosperity of kingdom. In a copper plate-inscription discovered in Joshimath, the Katyuri kings proudly style themselves as the *parambhakta*, i.e., the greatest devotees of Nanda Devi. After the downfall of the Katyuris in the late twelfth century, the region of Garhwal disintegrated into small territories ruled by petty chiefs from their *garh* (forts). During this time, prince Kanak Pal, hailing from the plains, visited Garhwal on a pilgrimage to Badrinath. He married the daughter of a chief ruling the small territory of Chandpur which lay on the route to the shrine. After his father-in-law's death, he became the new king. His descendant, Ajay Pal, was responsible for uniting the 52 scattered garhs into Garhwal. The bards who sing the history of the region claim that the princess whom Kanak Pal married was called Nanda, a reincarnation of Nanda Devi. As a result, the region of Chandpur is considered her mait[41], and the royal family of Garhwal as her people of mait.

The Raj Jat, or royal procession, is a ritualised dramatisation of the story of Nanda Devi where people from all over the state gather to escort Nanda from her mait in Chandpur to her husband's home in Kailash. The procession begins from Nauti village near the old fort of Chandpur and terminates at Lake Homkund, situated at the foot of Mount Trishul. Lasting a period of over three weeks and covering 280 kilometres, this yatra is supposed to be undertaken barefoot. With multiple stopovers, the Jat covers diverse landscapes ranging from villages, forest groves, alpine meadows, snowbound lakes and narrow ridges. Considering its significance and the scale of its organisation, this event is labelled the 'Himalayan Kumbh'. A once-in-a-generation affair and with significant resources invested in it, this is the most spectacular and the longest journey across rough terrain. Many small processions of Nanda Devi can be witnessed throughout Garhwal and Kumaon, but Raj Jat is distinct from them. The most significant difference is that it involves the participation of royals, giving it the name Raj Jat.

In the story, when Nanda feels unhappy and yearns to visit her natal home, she lays a curse on Rishau for ignoring her

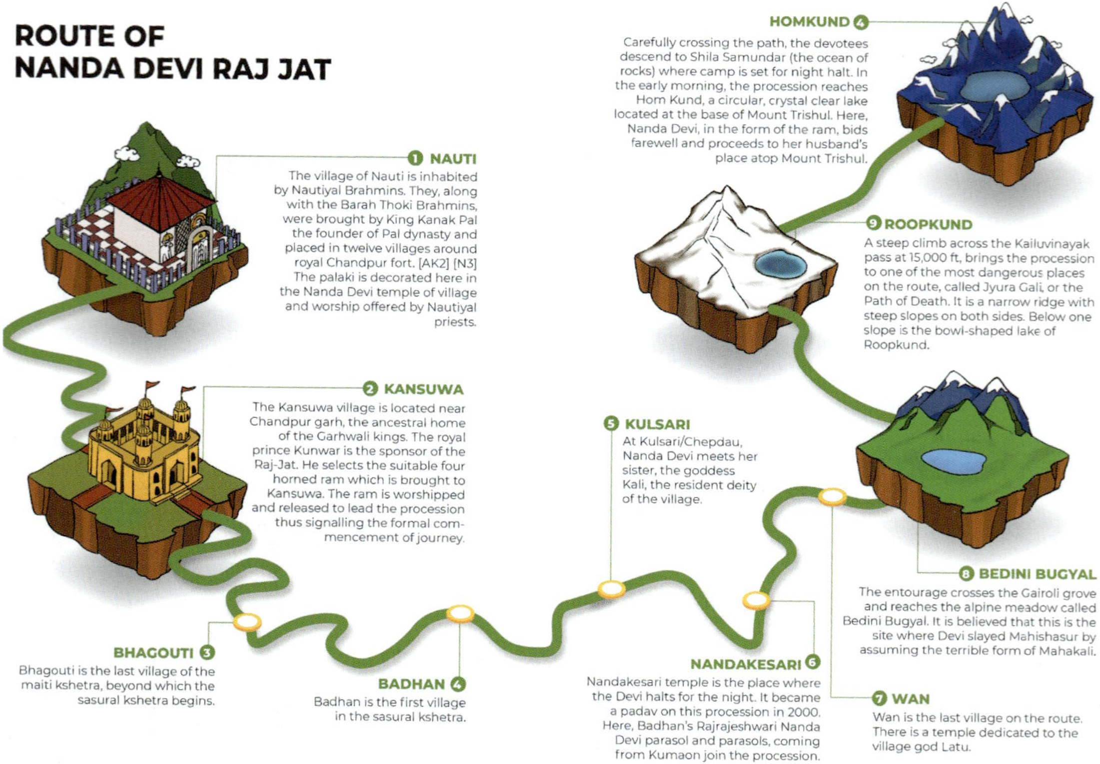

Figure 28 Map depicting the pilgrimage route of Nanda Devi Raj Jat

and putting her in such an inconvenient situation. Similarly, the time for organising the Raj Jat becomes apparent when mishaps befall the members of the royal family—their food is spoiled by maggots or their subjects suffer from disasters. In 1987, the Raj Jat was organised after a severe drought hit Garhwal; and in 2014, after the tragedy of the Kedarnath floods. The bad omens coincide with the miraculous birth of a rare four-horned ram (*chausingha maru*) within the boundaries of the former kingdom of Garhwal. To ensure prosperity and seek the blessing of the goddess, the royal family sponsors the procession and plays an important role in its successful completion.

Just like the twelve elder sages who tried to help Rishau emerge from his misfortunes caused by Nanda's anger, King Kanak Pal had invited twelve Brahmin families from the plains and settled them in twelve villages around the fort of Chandpur. Collectively called Barah Thoki Brahmins or Sarola Brahmins, each of them derives their title from the village they belong to: Semwals of Semgaon, Amolas of Amoli, Maithanis of Maithana, Dimris of Dimar, Nautiyals of Nauti, Thapliyals of Thapli, Khanduris of Khandura, Kothiyals of Kothi, Gairolas of Gairoli, Raturis of Ratura, Hatwals of Hatgaon, Chamolis of Chamoli and Semaltis of Semalta. Among them, the Nautiyals rank the highest as they were the *raj gurus* (royal preceptors), and the cooks of Panwar kings. As we read before, they were personally appointed by Nanda to look after the preparations during her visits.

Each lineage of Barah Thoki Brahmins chooses a representative who carries a parasol and joins the procession at predetermined locations. The procession, organised by Nautiyal Brahmins, starts at the Nanda Devi temple in their ancestral village of Nauti. Her palanquin is carved from mango wood and adorned with jewellery, clothes and flowers, and topped by a *mohra* (a mask or a human-like face usually made from silver) to give a human-like appearance to the deity. It is carried on the shoulders of priests from one village to the other. The selected four-horned ram is brought to this place and the Kunwar, the prince of the royal family, formally inaugurates the yatra. The ram is considered as Nanda Devi reborn and leads the party of priests and devotees throughout the procession, until the very end. It is followed by a royal parasol, then the parasol of Barah Thoki Brahmins and finally a crowd of hundreds of pilgrims.

The crowd grows as many local and village deities join the procession. Nanda Devi's palanquin gets surrounded by *chhantolis* (royal umbrella of the deity), or smaller *dolis,* that are covered in silver umbrellas. These belong to other regional gods and goddesses and, usually, each *patti* (a historical administrative unit) sends a chhantoli to the Raj Jat. Nanda is also accompanied by an oracle, who acts as a representative or spokesperson of the goddess. The goddess is supposed to possess the oracle, sending him into a trance. Nanda Devi then declares her will and communicates with her devotees through the oracle. The stopovers can last for a few hours to whole days. Offerings are made, blessings received and a public feast laid out for all.

As altitude is gained and the pilgrimage crosses the village of Badhan, the *sasural* region (in-law's house)—known as *sauras* in Garhwali—begins. The pilgrims would know when they have transitioned into sauras by noticing a change in the level of hospitality, or when they see parasols made of birch bark joining the procession. The people here, the highlanders, consider themselves representatives of Shiva and call Nanda *buari,* (daughter-in-law). Until now, the pilgrims were accustomed to a warm hospitality accorded by the locals with public feasts at every stop. But in sauras, things become different, and they must make their own arrangements for food and lodgings. It is not an easy task as the prices of basic commodities soar on higher altitudes. Nanda is the daughter of a lush valley where bamboo grows aplenty, while her husband's home is at the summit of a mountain where there is nothing "but snow to rear and snow to eat."[42] In her songs, Nanda sings that if a parasol made of bamboo arrives, it is from her mait, but if a parasol is lined with birch bark, it has come from her husband's home. Wan is the last inhabited village and, beyond it, wilderness begins. The upcoming climb is harsh and unpredictable, so women, children, and elders are advised not to proceed further.

From Wan, the parasol of Latu Devta, the brother of Nanda, leads the procession. The entourage crosses the Gairoli grove and reaches the alpine meadow of Bedni Bugyal. It is believed that this is the site where the Devi slayed Mahishasur[43] by assuming the terrible form of Mahakali. Shiva, then, had her bathe in the nearby Baitarani Kund from which she emerged in her natural form. Here, prayers are offered by the royal prince to the deceased King Jasdhawal and his own ancestors. The path leads to the grove of Patar Nachaniya where the dancing girls from Jasdhwal's entourage were turned into stone by an enraged Nanda Devi. A steep climb across the Kailuvinayak Pass at 15,000 feet brings the procession to one of the most dangerous places on the route; *Jyura Gali*, (the path of death). It is a narrow ridge with steep slopes on both sides. At the bottom of one slope is the bowl-shaped lake of Roopkund. Carefully crossing the path, the devotees descend to *Shila Samundar* (the ocean of rocks) where they set camp for the night. In the early morning, the procession reaches Homkund, a circular, crystal-clear lake located at the base of Mount Trishul. Here, the ram is sent off with offerings, a gesture to symbolise Nanda Devi proceeding towards her husband's abode atop Mount Trishul after bidding farewell to her people.

The devotees spend the night in Chandaniya Ghat. Then, by moving along the banks of the Nandakini river, they reach

Karnaprayag and again back to Nauti from where the crowd disperses for their homes. Many small annual processions of Nanda Devi occur all over Garhwal, but Raj Jat is the most significant of them all. Nanda is seen not only as the goddess who will grant the wishes of her devotees, but also as the loving daughter of her people who has to leave for her husband's home once every 12 years in a tearful journey. It is for her role as the daughter of every house in Garhwal and Kumaon that she is loved across the state of Uttarakhand, regardless of the variations in local culture.

> *'Bedu pako bara masa*
> *O Naraina kafal paako chaita, meri chhuila'*[44]
> (The fig tree fruits all-round the year,
> But O Narayana, Kafal berries only blossom in the month of Chaitra {April-May})

This song 'Bedu Pako Barah Masa' is one of the most popular folk songs of Uttarakhand and serves as the cultural anthem of all Pahadis. The verses describe the nostalgia experienced by a Kumaoni woman after witnessing the ripe Kafal[45] berries in springtime. It reminds her of fond memories of her natal home in Almora where, as a child, she had visited the famous Nanda Devi temple and roamed the iconic Lal Bazaar. The song is addressed to her husband, Narayana, with the lady pleading with him to take her back to her mait, where she will be lovingly welcomed.

The desire to visit one's parents' home finds constant expression in the songs sung by Pahadi women and has shaped the most celebrated pan-Indian myth of Goddess Parvati or Nanda Devi. The well-known story mentioned in the Shiva Purana and narrated in section Kedarnath of Chapter-2 tells of the rebirth of Sati as Parvati, the daughter of the Himalaya. When Shiva had immersed himself in deep meditation intending to carry on for aeons, the demon Taraka exploited the situation and obtained a boon from Brahma that he would only die at the hands of Shiva's son. Thinking himself to be invincible, he began harassing the Devas. Ultimately, Parvati married Shiva after he was impressed by her surviving the incredibly tough life of an ascetic for thousands of years. Their union resulted in the birth of Skand or Kartikeya, who went on to become the nemesis of the demon Taraka.

This account of Parvati's penance and the marriage of Shiva and Parvati deals primarily with the events of cosmic importance. The looming threat of the Asura Taraka to the world order lends an urgency to the reunion of Shiva and Parvati and makes the birth of Skanda, who would relieve the world of Taraka's oppression, the story's prime focus. The local adaptation of this tale in Pahadi culture, however, brings it much closer to the realities and lived experiences of ordinary hill women. Here, Nanda (Parvati's local name) takes birth not in the palace of the king of the mountains, but in the house of simple Himalayan peasants Hemant and Mainuli. In the Puranic version, Parvati herself chooses Shiva as her consort despite her parents' reservations and wins over Shiva with her ascetic prowess. But in the traditional societies of Garhwal and Kumaon where arranged marriages are a norm, Nanda's husband is selected by her parents and village elders.

Marriage has always been viewed as a significant and emotional event in a woman's life. Leaving her home and her loved ones whom she has known throughout her young life to move to an unfamiliar place, is a poignant event for her and her family. After her wedding, she becomes a *dhyani* (the married daughter of a village going to and tied to another village for the rest of her life). The story of Nanda Devi mirrors the experience of every Pahadi woman on the eve of her marriage. In Kailash, she leads an unhappy life. Bereft of any luxury or companionship, she longs for her home which she remembers was full of warmth and love. She symbolises the life of the women of the mountains, where men migrate to the plains in search of jobs leaving women alone to tend to the fields and raise children.

Soon after marriage, a Pahadi woman is expected to take on the mantle of domestic and agricultural duties working continuously for 14 to 16 hours a day. Waking up early in the morning, she cooks, cleans, and looks after the farm animals and her children. She travels miles to collect fuelwood and fodder, risking her life daily in the process for the chances of slipping on the steep slopes of hills are high; so are the chances of encountering a wild animal. She engages in back-breaking labour in the fields, doing everything except ploughing, a task which requires strength hence is carried out by the males. The only break from this repetitive cycle comes when she gets a chance to visit her mait, which comes around festivals like the annual Nanda Devi Jat. If only for a brief period, these visits give her a respite from her daily chores and some much-needed support from her parents. But soon, it's time to return to her sasural and resume the work. This teary-eyed departure for her husband's home and her longing for her own home forms the focus of the tale of Nanda Devi and is a constant theme in songs sung by womenfolk who relive their own memories of parting with their beloved mait.

7

BHOTIAS: THE ALPINE TRADERS

In Johar, a town in the Gori Ganga river valley high in the Himalaya, lived a woman of the local Shauka tribe.[46] Ganjuli Shaukyana was her name, and she was the wife of a Shauka merchant, Sunapati. The couple was childless, but not by choice. One day, she dreamt of the famous Bagnath temple of Baijnath and its deity, Lord Shiva, calling her to the temple on the day of the festival of Uttarayani. At the same time, the queen of the Katyuri dynasty living in the city of Vairat in the river valley of the middle Himalaya, also childless, had a similar dream. Both women, considering it a good omen, started off for Baijnath.

Wherever they went, the mood was festive. On the auspicious day of Uttarayani, both women went to the temple early in the morning to offer prayers and were drawn instinctively towards each other. They began talking and, when they realised that they were in a similar situation, the queen suggested a pact—if both women became pregnant, one with a boy and the other with a girl, they would wed them to each other. With the blessings of Lord Bagnath,

Figure 29 Meeting of Ganjuli and Queen at Bagnath temple

both were soon expecting. The queen gave birth to a boy and Ganjuli to a girl. The boy, named Malushahi, grew up and took over the kingdom after his father's death, while the girl, named Rajula, grew up to be a maiden of peerless beauty, enchanting everyone who laid eyes on her. By this time, the queen had forgotten her vow, but Ganjuli had not. She would often tell little Rajula the incredible story of her birth and the queen she had met. The story made a deep impression on young Rajula's mind, who soon grew obsessed with Malushahi and the idea of going to Vairat. But her father, Sunapati, did not wish to send his only child to a faraway land of Khasa people.

A trader named Vishayapala arrived with a marriage proposal after hearing of Rajula's beauty. He promised to give a lot of money and grains to Sunapati in return for Rajula's hand. Her father agreed and Vishayapala presented a traditional silver ornament to the unwilling Rajula as proof of their betrothal. After he left, promising to return with the wedding party, Rajula tried to reason with her parents and pleaded with them to not marry her to the uncivilised, wild and boorish clan of Vishayapal, asking to be married to Malushahi instead. But her father refused to listen. He dismissed Malushahi as a prince of people who know nothing about trade and ruling a land full of thorny grass and heat.

A few days later, Sunapati embarked on his customary trade journey to Tibet. Rajula, sensing an opportunity, ran away to meet Malushahi. Journeying across vast distances and navigating the challenging landscapes of mountains and valleys, Rajula finally reached the holy town of Baijnath. She offered prayers at the temple of Bagnath, imploring the God to fulfil her wish. She started for Vairat and, on her way, curiously observed the new culture of the lowlands, how differently people dressed and built houses, how different their language sounded. That night, Malushahi dreamed of a beautiful girl that made his heart flutter; before he knew it, he had fallen in love with her.

Next morning, Malushahi recounted his dream to his mother, the queen, vividly describing her distinctive features and her unique attire and ornaments. Hearing the description, the queen remembered the promise she had made to a Bhotia woman a long time ago. She was shaken, but dismissed this as mere coincidence.

Meanwhile, Rajula was causing a stir wherever she went. Lusting after her beauty, men confronted her and wanted to marry her then and there, but using her wits, Rajula managed to escape them all and finally reached Vairat. She managed to slip into the palace unseen and reached the chambers of Malushahi, who was asleep. When he opened his eyes, he saw the face he had dreamt of staring at him. He was astonished when he heard the tale Rajula told him. Rajula asked him to marry her before she was forced to marry Vishayapala. Since she had taken so much trouble to come and meet him, it was incumbent upon him to show similar resolve and take her away from her home as a true Kshatriya would. Rajula then began her journey towards home.

Malushahi resolved to win Rajula over. His mother agreed with a heavy heart, but instructed him to be careful, as the land was strange and so were the people and their customs. They were uncivilised and feared for practising black magic. Malushahi, taking some of his attendants who were familiar with the Shauka land and people, assumed the disguise of an ascetic and set off to bring Rajula. At Sunapati's house, the wedding preparations were in full swing when Malushahi's party gained entry as a band of monks who had come to bless the bride and the groom. They managed to reach Rajula, and Malushahi took her away. When Vishayapala received news of Rajula's disappearance, he grew furious. Gathering his men, he set off, chasing the couple. Being a native, he was familiar with the terrain and started gaining on them. But with the blessings of Lord Bagnath, a mist suddenly descended on the mountains and confused Vishayapala and his soldiers. The couple soon left the Shauka lands behind and were married in a grand ceremony. They lived happily ever after.

In some versions, this tale ends in tragedy. In one, when Malushahi tries to meet Rajula, he is poisoned by Vishayapala and dies, while Rajula has to wed Vishayapala against her wishes. This love ballad, propagated over generations through oral tradition, was first printed in a book titled *Himalayan Folklore* by T.C. Gairola, a civil servant who, along with missionary E. Sherman Oakley, collected and published English translations of prominent Himalayan folktales, including those in Garhwali and Kumaoni. The

Figure 30 Rajula and Malushahi fleeing while being chased by Vishayapala's men

story was also dramatised for the stage by Mohan Upreti who is remembered for his contribution to the revitalisation of Kumaoni folk culture. The tale is a classic ballad and sheds light on many cultural aspects of the Shauka people, the Bhotia tribe of Johar Valley and their relations with the neighbouring Pahadi people of the lowlands. Many cultural and economic traits of the Shaukas highlighted in the story continued to exist until recent times.

Malushahi was a Katyuri prince, a Khasa or Pahadi, while Rajula was a Bhotia of the Shauka tribe. 'Bhot' means north, and it is a southern Himalayan custom to name people residing in or coming from the north as Bhotia. However, Bhotia is a misnomer, a practice started by the British who clubbed different ethnic tribes engaged in Trans-Himalayan trade with Tibet under the blanket term of Bhotia, which the community does not like. Spread across three districts of Uttarakhand, these tribes live in the upper reaches of seven different river valleys of the Greater Himalaya near the Indo-Tibetan border. In Uttarkashi district, the Jadh Bhotia tribe lives in the Nelang and Jadung valleys. In Chamoli district, the Bhotia tribes of Marchhas and Tolchhas occupy Mana and Niti valleys and use these passes for trade and pastoral activities. In Pithoragarh, the Shaukas reside in Johar Valley while the Rongpa or Rungs inhabit Darma, Byans and Chaudans valley. These seven river valleys are part of the

Ganga and Kali River systems spread across Garhwal and Kumaon.

In terms of ethnicity, Bhotias do not accept the Tibetan origin ascribed to them by anthropologists, but trace their

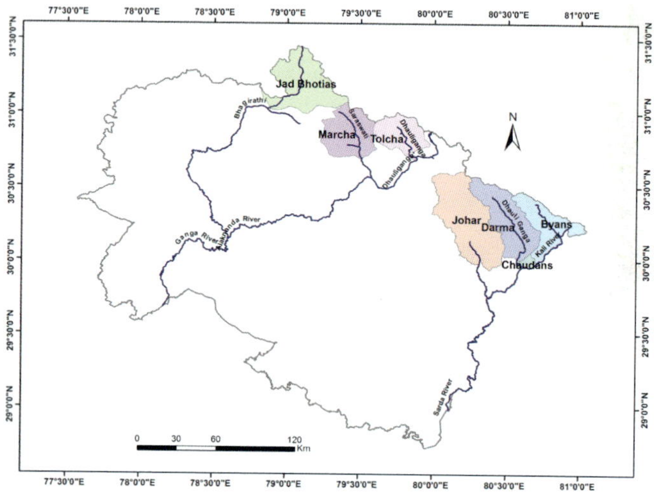

Figure 31 Map showing the spread of Bhotia communities in different river valleys

origin to the Rajput clans, Chandravanshi and Raghuvanshi.[47] As per the lore, their ancestors migrated to Tibet several centuries ago and after living there for several generations, they returned to their present locations in the Himalaya. However, due to intermingling with the Tibetans (called Hun Desh or Huniya in local parlance) and marrying their women, cultural influences and characteristics of the Tibetan people became more pronounced in them over time. Socially, caste

Figure 32 (a, b and c) Jad Bhotia couple during the opening of Gangotri Dham; Marccha woman from Mana village at Badrinath; Shauka woman of Johar Valley

divisions among Bhotias are not as strong as those prevalent in the society of the middle Himalaya and Gangetic plains. The community carries typical surnames of Thakur, Rawat and Chauhan and, in recent times, marriages with Pahadi Rajputs have become more common. Many carry surnames which indicate the name of the village they belong to. For example, those with the Tolia surname hail from Toli village, Martolia from Martoli village etc.

All tribes are predominantly Hindus, with some Buddhist influences.[48] The Jad tribe residing near Gangotri and Marchha near Badrinath are enthusiastic participants in the ceremonies of the opening and closing of the gates of Char-Dham. In Badrinath, before the closing of the gates in winters, the main image of Vishnu is put in a supine position and a thick blanket is laid over it. The Marchha women of Mana village especially weave this warm blanket for the lord. The local deity of Mana, Ghantakarna, is considered the *anga-rakshaka* (bodyguard) of Lord Badrinath. Similarly, the Shaukas and the Rongpa inhabit the region dubbed Adi-Kailash that contains the historic route towards Kailash-Mansarovar located in Tibet. The festival of Nanda Ashtami dedicated to Goddess Nanda is celebrated by them with great fervour.

Trans-Himalayan Trade with Tibet

Although these seven tribes had little contact with each other due to being separated by mountains, a common culture developed over time. This similarity could be said to arise from living in the same geographical and climatic conditions, making it necessary to adapt and develop a new economic mode of living. Rajula's father, Sunapati, was a trader who used to be away from home for long stretches on his annual trip to Tibet along with fellow traders. Trade was the backbone of the Bhotia economy and the secret behind their prosperity despite the harsh climate and the barren land on which they lived.

In mainstream societies where agriculture is the main occupation, wealth and power is measured in terms of ownership of land. But in Bhotia society, where land is poor and often snow bound, the wealth is evaluated in terms of the size of livestock, comprising sheep, goats, yak, and *jubu* (a cross-breed of the Tibetan yak and Indian cow).

A wealthy trader could sometimes own thousands of animals that not only provided meat and wool but were also used as pack animals to carry goods back and forth across mountain passes. The Pahadis inhabited relatively low mountains and river valleys and could afford to rely on the fruits of agriculture. The Bhotia homeland, however, remained under snow, six to twelve inches deep, for half the year from November till May. This restricted agriculture to one short season—sowing in June and harvesting in September—not enough to sustain their population. Consequently, Bhotias learned to adapt by being semi-nomadic; they would stay at 2–3 different locations throughout the year. Movement became a constant feature of their life and culture. For the short growing season in the summer, they lived in their summer dwellings in the highlands. Here, peasants tilled the land, while the shepherds of the community, known as *anwals,* took their animals to graze in the high-altitude meadows blooming with fresh nutritious grass. When the snow would start falling and the weather became too cold, the community migrated en masse with their livestock to their winter dwellings called *gunshas* positioned in the lower reaches of the same river valley.

This practice of seasonal migration with livestock and possessions to the highlands in the summer and back to the lowlands in the winter is called transhumance. In the opposite direction of mait, at the head of the river valley, lies the mountain pass beyond which lay Tibet (Huniya), ethnically and culturally different from the Indian Pahadi people on the other side of the Himalaya.

The Bhotias—with their location at the junction of these two cultural spheres, the advantage of being acclimated to the high-altitude climate and their knowledge of navigating difficult passes—converted their geographic disadvantage into an opportunity. Although their looks and language greatly resembled Tibetans, their customs and religion were greatly influenced by the Pahadi neighbours to the south. Acting as cultural middlemen between these two communities of Tibetans and Pahadis, they soon acquired a monopoly over the trade between the Uttarakhand region and Tibet.

During winters, the Bhotias spent their time in the lower hills, in the company of Pahadi dwellers. When the Pahadi peasants harvested the winter crops, the surplus grain would be exchanged with the Bhotias for salt and wool. With the onset of summers, they migrated back to their mait. The snow on the mountain passes would not melt till June-July. After the passes became navigable again, an agent from Tibet would arrive for a recce before opening the trade routes. His main aim was to ensure that the Bhotia lands were free from plague and to check if there had been a bountiful harvest in the lower region. If satisfied by the reports of their agents, the Tibetan officials would declare the routes open. Loading grains purchased from Pahadi farmers onto their pack animals, the Bhotia traders would set off along the river valleys while the women and children looked after agriculture in the villages. After crossing into Tibet through the mountain pass, traders would offer sugar cakes, woollen cloths, the green tops of fir trees and grains etc. as a tribute to the Tibetan authorities governing the pass. From thereon, they would move to the nearest *mandi* (trade depot) where the exchange of goods would take place. After staying for 2–3 months in Tibet, the train of merchants would return using the same route before the snow started falling at the end of October.

Figure 33 A high altitude Bhotia village

The temple of Bagnath is located at the confluence of river Gomti and Saryu at Bageshwar, and Shiva is worshipped as the Lord of the Tiger (*Bagh* means tiger). The temple plays a pivotal role in the story of the Rajula-Malushahi. The fertile Katyur valley of Bageshwar used to be the capital of the Katyuri kings. They were the first major dynasty to emerge in these mountains, and with time splintered into small principalities ruled by local chieftains, Vairat was one of them. On the auspicious date of Makar Sankranti, when the sun starts its northern journey from the southern hemisphere, the festival of Uttarayani is celebrated every year. It is one of the biggest festivals of Kumaon, when people would come from near and far to pray at the Bagnath temple and take a dip in the holy confluence of rivers Gomti and Saryu. Earlier, one of the biggest attractions of the fair were the trade marts set up by the Bhotia traders who would have returned from their annual trip to Tibet. They would sell their wares—salt to the locals and borax, wool and gold dust to the other merchants who attended the festival from all over Kumaon and nearby plains.

Thus, the trans-Himalayan trade with Tibet was integrated with the annual practice of transhumance by the Bhotias. Tibet, a cold desert, was completely dependent on the import of grains for its food security. Edwin Atkinson, a civil servant, noted in his gazetteer that, 'If passes were to be closed even for a single season it would lead to famine in Tibet.'[49] The items of import—salt, borax, gold dust and wool—were all high value–low volume items. Salt was always in high demand on the Indian side of mountains since the salt obtained from the coastal regions could not reach the mountains or was unsustainably expensive. In contrast, the salt mined from Tibet and brought by the Bhotias was far cheaper. The cold climate of Tibet was suitable to produce fine wool and was brought by the Bhotias for self-consumption. The dresses of Bhotia men and women were all made of raw wool either brought from Tibet or locally produced, and then dexterously woven by skilled Bhotia women into a variety of clothes. Borax was in great demand in Europe where it was chiefly used as a fluxing agent in metal soldering, i.e., for cleaning the surface of metal pieces before being joined through melting.

Until the twentieth century, Tibet remained the only source of borax, which was the most lucrative item of the Bhotia trade.

Among all the tribes, the Shaukas of the Johar Valley were the most significant. They enjoyed certain privileges over others, like choosing the *mandis* (the traditional Indian market where goods are bought and sold) for their trade etc., accorded to them by the Tibetan authorities. The reason behind this special status lay in the fact that the route on which they operated—the Unta Dhura pass at the head of the Gori Ganga—was the oldest, making the Shauka traders the most experienced traders in business. Additionally, the volume of trade was very high on this route in comparison to other routes. During British rule, the Rungs of the Darma valley came close for the first time, achieving a level of trade and prosperity similar to the Shaukas, but it was short-lived.

The Kingdom of Tibet had always fascinated the British, who were much interested in gaining a share in the lucrative trade of Pashmina shawls and Chinese tea, the premium products of Tibet. As the East India Company consolidated its rule over Bengal, a war broke out in 1772 between Bhutan, a Tibetan protectorate and Cooch Behar, a princely state bordering Bengal and Bhutan. The king of Cooch Behar appealed to the East India company for military aid. Sensing an opportunity, the Company, led by the first Governor-General Warren Hastings, intervened, and defeated the Bhutanese forces.

This victory proved to be impactful as they received a letter from the 6th Panchem Lama, the political head of Tibet, to treat Bhutan leniently. Eager to establish trade relations with Tibet and through them with China, Hastings dispatched a mission in 1774. It was headed by George Bogle, a diplomat, adventurer and Hasting's private secretary, with the purpose to establish diplomatic relations with Tibet. Bogle's mission was a moderate success. He stayed in Tibet for five months and sent a great deal of his observations about Tibetan culture and manners in his reports to Hastings. A person of tact and charisma, he soon became friends with the 6th Panchem Lama who promised to explore opportunities of greater trade with the company. But the plans did not materialise due to the death of Lama in 1779 and of Bogle in the succeeding year. Company tried to regain its position in Tibet by dispatching Lieutenant Samuel Turner, Hastings's cousin on a diplomatic mission to Tibet in 1783. But Turner could not do much to advance the company's position as the new Panchem Lama was an infant.

In 1811, Thomas Manning became the first company agent to secure entry into Lhasa, the seat of the famed Lamas of Tibet. The Chinese authorities, alarmed by their neighbours falling prey to the influence of colonial powers, soon closed their borders including Tibet to all foreigners in 1850. All three company agents left detailed accounts of their travels, but it was Samuel Turner's book, *An Account of an Embassy to the Court of Teshoo Lama in Tibet*, published in

1800, that remained a standard reference book for British authorities for the next 75 years, since the journals of the other two diplomats were not published until 1876. Despite their efforts, many regions of Tibet, especially in the south, remained unexplored and blank on the map.

The British interest in Tibet stemmed from commercial and political imperatives. The Company was very much interested in the lucrative trade of Pashmina shawls and wanted to divert it from Ladakh (which had the monopoly over it) to its territories in Garhwal and Kumaon. However, the most immediate need was a strategic one, for Russia was increasingly advancing and colonising the Central Asian regions bordering Tibet. The British were worried about rumours surrounding the growing closeness between the Dalai Lama and the Czar of Russia. They wanted to keep Tibet out of Russian influence and as a neutral buffer between the Russian and British empires. This tussle with Russia for influence in Tibet and Central Asia was dubbed the 'Great Game'. To gain an advantage in this rivalry, the Company had to solve its problem of knowing so little about Tibetan geography and terrain.

Although Tibet had closed its borders to outsiders, the trade routes with the neighbouring states of Ladakh, Bushahr, Kumaon and Nepal were still in operation as trade was critical for the survival of Tibet's economy. The British had, by then, won Garhwal and Kumaon from the Gurkhas and, in the reorganisation of territory afterwards, had kept all the important passes leading to Tibet under its control. The Company's search for a solution landed them on the doorstep of the Johar Valley, the home of the Shauka community, historically the most prosperous among the Bhotia tribes. But the fortunes of a certain Johari named Nain Singh Rawat were far from great. A teacher at a British school in the village of Milam, Rawat was poor and debt-ridden. But his sharp intellect and quickness to learn were recognised by Thomas George Montgomerie, a colonel working on the Trigonometric Survey of India engaged in measuring and mapping the Himalaya. Denied access to Tibet, he had proposed working with the native Indians, who would survey Tibet on behalf of the company. One among many 'natives' selected for this task, Nain Singh was trained in the intricacies of cartography and mapping at the office of the Trigonometric Survey in Dehradun. There, he learnt handling and operating delicate instruments like sextants; techniques of surveying and collecting data including measuring altitude based on the boiling point of water and calculating distances based on the pace of his walk.

In 1865, Nain Singh, along with his fellow native surveyors, started for Tibet through Nepal disguised as Buddhist monks from Bushehr. Through his charisma and smooth-talking, Nain Singh managed to slip past the suspicious eyes of Tibet authorities even when his fellow companions could not. Once in Tibet, he had to be extremely careful lest he and his instruments were discovered by the officials, for the penalty if caught would be nothing short of certain death by beheading. He noted every piece of geographical information he could gather throughout his journey in the form of Buddhist hymns concealed in scrolls which, in turn, were hidden in prayer wheels. To outsiders, he gave the impression of being a pious Buddhist silently whispering his prayers when, in reality, he was counting each of his steps to calculate the distance from one town to another. The wealth of information he brought back astounded the British officials. His expedition not only helped fill in the hitherto blank areas of the map but also confirmed Lhasa's exact location and that the Tsang-po and the Brahmaputra are one river. He covered of over 1,900 kilometres—which totalled two-and-a-half million footsteps—and measured the position, altitude and other geographical details of every hill, river, town, and mart he came across on his misson. Narrowly escaping exposure several times, his journey was full of adventures and encounters. Thus, the Great Game between Britain and Russia over the control of central Asia triggered the mapping and exploration of the Himalaya in which the Bhotias, especially Nain Singh Rawat, played a substantial role.

The British colonial rule from 1815—after the defeat of Gurkhas and the annexation of the region by the British—continued until India's independence in 1947. It affected the trade with Tibet in several ways. For one, the customary mode of exchange—the barter system, where grain was exchanged for other items—got replaced with money-based exchange. The borax trade with Tibet remained highly profitable during the early phase of colonial rule as Tibet remained the only source. Borax brought at the cost of ₹1 from Tibet was sold by the Bhotias at ₹8 in the Bageshwar mart, which was resold in cities of the plains at eight times the price and was also exported to Europe. In 1858, from Calcutta alone, 10,896 maunds of borax was exported to Europe.'[50] But the trade was dealt a blow when an alternate method of creating borax from boric acid was discovered by scientists thus reducing its demand from Europe. In contrast, wool trade saw a boost, with the setting up of new textile mills by the British in Kanpur, present-day Uttar Pradesh. The wool brought over by Bhotia traders from Tibet was sold to millers after keeping some for self-consumption. The demand increased steadily in the last quarter of the ninteenth century, so mill agents started giving an advance to Bhotia traders to bring a certain quantity of wool from Tibet to meet their demands. The burgeoning trade faced hurdles with the occurrence of the First World War (1914-1918) which made the goods scarce and caused a sharp increase in their prices. This led to lesser volumes of export to Tibet and subsequently lesser goods imported so the profits of the traders declined. From then onwards, the trade with Tibet started showing diminishing trends.

The trans-Himalayan trade came to an abrupt stop after the borders were declared closed by the Indian government post the Chinese aggression in 1962. The sudden severance of the main artery of the Bhotia economy plunged the community into a severe economic crisis. However, being an industrious and close-knit community, the Bhotias successfully sailed through this catastrophe. The excellence gained in the woollen textile sector helped hundreds of families to migrate to alternate livelihoods during the worst period. The cold climate of the mountains is suitable for producing wool while also necessitating the weaving of woollen clothing as protection against the biting cold. The Bhotia women and the elderly who did not accompany their trading members to Tibet engaged in wool-shearing, cleaning, spinning and weaving a variety of products ranging from coarse wool-made carpets to scarfs made of finely woven Pashmina.

With time, the educated youth found employment with the government, while village-based youth engaged themselves in the service-based hospitality sector, acting as guides and porters and selling rare herbs and plants collected from the wild. It is a testimony to the industriousness and adaptability of the Bhotias that despite facing an economic disaster during the '60s, they became the most prosperous and educated scheduled tribe of Uttarakhand.

8

TONS VALLEY: REALM OF THE ORACLE KINGS

On a clear winter morning, a priest wearing only a loincloth emerged from a ceremonial bath in the ice-cold water of a Himalayan spring. The temperature was close to freezing, but the priest gave no indication of discomfort because one, he was the priest of the divine King Mahasu, and two, his *panti* (ritual duty) was about to start. Being allowed to perform panti was a privilege bestowed upon very few. Only specific lineages among selected clans of the Brahmin community were eligible for it. The chosen one had to follow a strict code of conduct—maintain celibacy, limit one's dietary intake to a few items, and always do one's own cooking. The spring was located within the temple premises but some distance from the main shrine. As the priest started his upward journey to awaken the god and start his daily worship, a government car halted a little way from the temple. It was the vehicle of the *naib-tehsildar* (a land revenue officer), on his way to collect dues from defaulters who had taken a loan from the government and had not paid back yet. The priest was

Figure 34 The principle temple of Mahasu Devta at Hanol

also one of them. He was approached by the tehsildar and ordered to either pay the money or be arrested. The temple officials and local people tried to educate the tehsildar in the importance of the work that the priest was doing, and that he could arrest the priest after he'd completed his duties to Mahasu Devta. But the tehsildar, a man from the plains and unaware of local customs, arrested the priest, put him in the jeep, and drove off to the administrative centre of Tiuni.[51]

On the way, the driver lost control of the jeep and hit a parapet above the gorge. Everyone was badly injured but, miraculously, the priest was unscathed. An ambulance was called for the injured, while the priest was taken to Tiuni in another car to face the civil court. However, the local people had already reached the court and paid the money on behalf of the priest. He was let off, free to complete his duties. The tehsildar, who had interrupted Mahasu's rituals, suffered a stroke two weeks later and no modern medicine or doctor could cure him of his condition. His local driver, aware of the chain of incidents, diagnosed the cause of his pitiful condition to the curse of Mahasu Devta. He advised his master to ask Mahasu Devta for forgiveness. The tehsildar was produced before Mahasu on a stretcher at the temple at Hanol, the principal seat of the god, where he begged for forgiveness. The oracle of Mahasu, sitting near the dark antechamber, started shaking and went into a trance, indicating that he had become possessed by Mahasu. Through his mouth, Mahasu accepted Tehsildar's apologies and communicated the remedy. The offender was to seek forgiveness with his entire family and a goat was to be sacrificed as recompense. The tehsildar duly complied and recovered from his condition. This strange place, where Gods act as kings and pronounce their decisions through an oracle, has since long fascinated and terrified all political forces—the Garhwal kings, the British and modern Indian bureaucracy—that sought to control and administer this region.

In the extreme north west of Uttarakhand from the icy heights of Bandarpoonch range emerge two streams called Rupin and Supin. They meet at the small hamlet of Netwar and the combined river is henceforth known by the name of

Tons. It carves its way through the rugged mountains and just short of exiting the mountains at Kalsi, it merges with the waters of Yamuna coming from the opposite direction. Although, at the time of the confluence, Tons carries more volume of water, due to cultural significance, the combined river that flows into the plains of Dehradun is known as Yamuna. These two rivers define the oval-shaped territory of Jaunsar-Bawar, with Tons marking its northern and western boundaries and Yamuna its eastern and southern boundaries. As the name denotes, the division of Jaunsar-Bawar is made of two distinct subdivisions—Jaunsar and Bawar. The ridge of Lokhandi, the highest point of the region, acts as a divider between the two, with Jaunsar comprising $2/3^{rd}$ of the division and Bawar the remaining $1/3^{rd}$. The land lying upstream of Bawar and enclosed by Greater Himalaya, is called Rawain and is considered as a transition between Jaunasar-Bawar and Garhwal proper.

The culture of these regions, demarcated by river Tons and Yamuna, revolve around the institution of divine kingship, where the deity is perceived as a king who rules his kingdom and subjects through a well-defined bureaucracy with key political functions spread across the social castes and lineages. For instance, he enforces his decisions through an oracle, manages his treasury and runs the royal affairs through a minister while his tales and history are recited by bard-drummers.

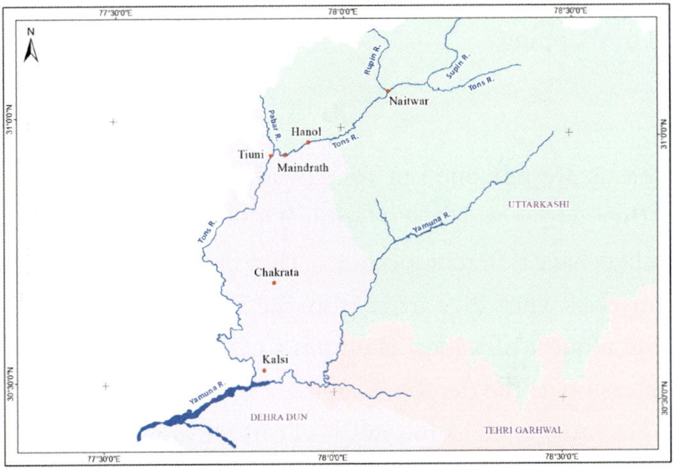

Figure 35 Map depicting the territory of Jaunsar-Bawar with major locations

The region of Jaunsar-Bawar is synonymous with Mahasu Devta although their influence extends far beyond its borders into Jubbal, Sirmaur and Rohru areas of neighbouring Himachal Pradesh. Other divine kings of the upper reaches of Tons Valley include King Karna of Netwar (although he is named after the popular figure of *Mahabharata*, the deity bears little resemblance to him); Someshwar of Jakhol, Kush Devta of Kot Gaon and many more. These kings are often accompanied by their generals or bodyguards, who are worshipped in their own right. For instance, Pokhu Devta is the general of King Karna. Although being the tutelary deities of their respective region, the territorial boundaries of these divine kings are not sharply defined, instead are fluid and overlapping.

Mahasus are not one but four brothers, and it is only one brother who resides at Hanol. The other three Mahasu brothers have different locations. They choose these locations themselves when they arrive from the fabled land of Kashmir at the request of a local Brahmin to free the land from the oppression of the demon Kirmir.

The story goes as follows[52]—Lord Shiva was engaged in meditation at Kailash when a demon started pestering him. Angry, Shiva created four warriors from his body to catch the demon. The warriors chased the demon throughout the land of Uttarakhand. At Kharamba, his feet were chopped off; at Mundoli, he was divested of his head; at a ridge which divides Jaunsar and Bawar, his arms were cut off. Finally, the demon escaped north into higher snowbound terrain where his blood and tears flowed down as river Tons. After the task was completed, Shiva ordered the four warriors to rest at the bottom of a lake in Kashmir. Once, an argument broke out between Shiva and his eldest, Kartikeya, who accused his mother, Parvati, of favouring Ganesha over him. Shiva reminded him that she is his mother, the one who gave birth to his form. In anger, Kartikeya cut off his flesh in four parts and threw them in a lake. Four Nagas were inhabiting that lake, who ate Kartikeya's flesh and from their belly emerged the four Mahasu brothers. The four warriors, created by Shiva previously, became their deputy generals.

After the Pandavas left for their heavenly abode, demons began ruling the Earth. The demon Kirmir terrorized the land of Jaunsar. There, in the small village of Maindrath, lived Una Bhat with his family and clan. Kirmir killed and ate several members of his family. Una wanted revenge and resolved to do whatever it took to kill the demon. One night, he dreamed of a handsome man near a lake in Kashmir. The next day, Una Bhat started his journey to the place in his dream. The only trouble was, he did not know where the fabled land of Kashmir lay. On his way, at a place called Hatkoti, he met a Naga who had been to Kashmir. At first, the Naga tried to dissuade him by telling him the difficulties which lay in Una's way. But when he saw that nothing could shake Una's resolve, he blessed him and gave him directions to Kashmir. He told Una to check if he had indeed reached the right place by throwing a lock of his hair and spitting in the water. If the two things changed form in some way, it would mean that he had arrived in the magical land of Kashmir. Una followed his directions and reached a lake where, upon touching the water, locks of his hair became snakes and his spittle became oysters, proving that he had finally reached his destination. He waited near the bank of the lake and saw Pabsik Mahasu emerging from the water. He went to him and begged for his help. Seeing Una's pitiful condition, he and his brothers agreed to help him, but told Una that

Figure 36 Mahasu brothers emerging from land at Una Bhat's request

they would only arrive at the appropriate time. They give him a magical container, a few grains of rice and bid him farewell with specific instructions regarding the preparations that needed to be made for their arrival.

Una Bhat eagerly returned home and immediately set to work. He readied a virgin field and employed a bachelor youth who ploughed the field with calves that had never been yoked before. Upon touching the land, the wooden plough turned into gold, its blade silver. Five furrows were dug and the rice grains given by Mahasu were spread across those furrows. The Mahasu brothers emerged from one furrow each. Their mother, Dyoladi, emerged from the fifth. Mahasu's deputies and *bir* (warriors) also emerged after the brothers. Eager to bring the Mahasus to his land, Una had performed the ritual a day before the appointed time. Due to this oversight, the eldest brother, Bautha, hurt his leg while emerging from the Earth. Next, Pabsik's eyes were injured, while Basik had his hearing impaired. Only Chalda emerged unscathed. The four brothers set out to complete the task for which they had come. They challenged the demon Kirmir to a fight and chased him across the region. Finally, at the ridge Bhujakoti, which separates Jaunsar and Bawar, they slew the demon. As part of claiming the kill, they divided the demon's body among themselves. No matter how they divided, one extra piece was always left. This extra piece of flesh escaped and ran towards the snowbound mountains, all the while shouting at Mahasu, "This region belongs to you now.

Figure 37 Mahasu brothers chasing the demon Kirmir

But leave the upper regions permanently under snow to us demons!" Saying so, it disappeared. The Mahasus decided to permanently reside in the territory they had liberated from the oppression of Kirmir. They selected the site of Hanol where a temple of Vishnu already stood. They challenged Vishnu, the resident deity, of the temple to a contest—that whoever could produce more gold would win and the other would leave that place. The brothers won and Vishnu left his seat, taken up by the victors and it became the principal temple of the Mahasu sect.

The territory won over from Kirmir was divided among the four brothers and their deputies. The temple of Hanol serves as the seat of Bautha Mahasu, who chose to permanently station himself at the temple due to his leg injury and rule the entire arca under Mahasu influence. Pabsik or Pavasi Mahasu has his seat at Thadiyar, on the opposite side of the river, overlooking Hanol. He was tasked to rule the territories lying on the right bank of the Tons, in the state of Himachal Pradesh. Basik Mahasu is seated at Maindrath, about 10 kilometres from Hanol, and looks after the territory on the left bank of the Tons. Basik Mahasu is seated at Maindrath, about 10 kilometres from Hanol, and looks after the territory on the right bank of the Tons. Maindrath is the seat of the mother of the four Mahasu Devtas, Dyoladi Devi. Chalda, the fittest of them all, was given the task to tour the whole territory. He would tour the territory on one side for 12 years and cross to the territory on the other bank for the next 12 years. He would fight off aggression from other enemies and divinities and work to expand the domain of Mahasu. Today, the brothers rule from their respective temples, which are thronged by their devotees from near and afar. Chalda Mahasu is perpetually on tour, crossing and recrossing the Tons river every 12 years, gracing the people across the Mahasu territory with his presence.

JAUNSAR-BAWAR AND THE MAHABHARATA

A closer study of story of Una Bhat and the arrival of the Mahasu to Jaunsar-Bawar highlights the ways in which the Mahasu brought change to the Jaunsari society. One important trend it subtly indicates is the transition of Jaunsari society from being Pandava-centric culture (like adjoining Garhwal) to a Mahasu-centric culture. The Mahasus replaced the Pandavas as the most popular hero figures. In the classical version of *Mahabharata*, it is Bhima who slays the demon Kirmir, but in the Jaunsari version, Pandavas have left Earth, giving demons an opportunity to spread terror once again. It is to fill this vacuum that four brothers arrive from Kashmir with their mother Dyoladi to slay the demon Kirmir. The parallels with the Pandavas are striking. Five brothers with their mother versus four brothers with their mother and an uncertain paternity. Thus, with the coming of the Mahasus, a difference emerged from the neighbouring Garhwal where Pandava-worship is very common. There, Pandava *nrityas,*[53] a ritual dance drama, are organised in villages where the Pandavas and their wife, Draupadi, and mother, Kunti, possess people and bless the gatherings. In contrast, in Jaunsar-Bawar, it is the Mahasus, their deputies and mother Dyoladi who routinely possess people during public festivals. Still, some influence of the *Mahabharata* remains in Jaunsar. It is observed in connection with geography and kinship patterns.

Pandav Vivah - Absent in the adjoining areas of Himachal and Garhwal, the social practice of fraternal polyandry—a woman with more than one husband—was unique to the Valley of Tons. Called *Pandav Vivah* locally, it was believed to be established by the Pandavas on their visit to this region during their exile. Major Campbell, the magistrate of the Chakrata cantonment, had studied this institution closely. As per him, the polyandry practised in the region was 'fraternal' in nature and was practised within the family, i.e., the set of husbands taking a common wife had to be related as brothers (either sons of the same mother or having a common father). Campbell attributed the origin of this practice to the economic necessity of preventing the further splitting of a landholding within the family and keeping the family intact by preventing disputes. With the average size of a family of five, each family owned very small landholdings, i.e., less than three acres of land. The produce from meagre arable land could not support the small population of Jaunsar-Bawar. Despite small consumption, calculated as 12 pounds of unhusked grain per person a day, in the bad years when the monsoon failed, the food grains still had to be imported from the plains. To survive in the hostile geography, another sustainable mode of living had to be developed. As the gazetteer noticed, a Jaunsari is as much a shepherd as a tiller of land.[54] Hence, the Jaunsari developed a mixed practice of agriculture as well as pastoralism and kept a large flock of livestock which provided much necessary nutrition during lean winter months when agriculture ceased. The male members of the family travelled with sheep or livestock for months to graze as long as the season allowed. The other family members, like the other brothers or the womenfolk, stayed in the house to till the fields and carry out other household chores.

Social identity - Jaunsar also has its own unique version of the *Mahabharata*. In this version, the Kauravas are not 100, but 60. The Tons is taken as the line dividing the region into two opposite factions called *Saathi* and *Pansi*. The people residing on these opposite banks believe that their ancestors fought on the side of the Kauravas and the Pandavas during the eighteen-day war. The Saathi fought alongside the Kauravas, hence their name Saathi, derived from the Hindi word *saath*, meaning sixty, while Pansi (from five) had fought on the side of the Pandavas. The people residing on one bank did not prefer *roti-beti ka rishta* (kinship relations) with those opposite the shore. The rivalry between the two factions is displayed during the annual festival of Bissu Mela held in April. Men from both sides enact a mock battle and throw arrows at each other. They wear 40-feet long pyjamas folded many times over as protection from any injuries.

Localisation of events- Some places in Jaunsar-Bawar are said to be sites where events from the *Mahabharata* took place. A few hours away from Chakrata is the small village of Lakhamandal. Local people believe that this is the place where the Lakshagriha, or 'house of lac', episode of the *Mahabharata* took place. Kauravas, out of their jealousy and hatred, plotted to finish the Pandavas by constructing a palace made of lac, an inflammable substance, and making the Pandavas, who were touring this region, stay there. When the Kauravas set fire to the palace, the Pandavas, who had been informed of the conspiracy, escaped via a secret tunnel.

After the brothers had divided the territory among themselves, the next step was to create an effective system to manage and run their kingdom smoothly. Since Una Bhat was the one who had invited them, it was his responsibility to ensure that Mahasu were properly taken care of. Una appointed his three sons to look after their affairs. The eldest son would take care of ritual offerings and would be called *Deo Pujya* (priest), a name to be carried on by his descendants. The second son was given the clan name of *Rajput*, and his task was to manage the temple affairs and the daily ringing of the temple bells. The third son, Bajgi, was responsible for playing the drums and being the keeper of Mahasu's genealogy and tales. The three sons of the tale correspond to the three communities of Brahmins, Rajputs and Bajgis, who comprise the present-day Jaunsari society. Certain clans within each caste perform specific functions and exercise a degree of sacramental control over the affairs of Mahasu and run the kingdom on his behalf.

The key posts and roles of this social bureaucracy are:

1. ***Mali* (Oracle)**–Spokesperson of the Mahasus. The Mahasu briefly inhabits the body of his oracle to speak through him and pronounce his decisions to his subjects. Possession of one oracle must be authenticated by other oracles for genuineness.
2. ***Deo Pujya* (Priest)**–Has to follow a very strict code of conduct and purification to perform his duty towards

Mahasu Devta. His duty starts before sunrise and continues until sunset and includes various rituals and worship.

3. ***Wazir* (Minister)**–The task of running the kingdom in the name of Mahasu is performed by the Wazir. He is the executive of the divine king. Among the group of officials, he is the most powerful and exerts considerable influence in the Mahasu territory, which translates into electoral clout in current politics. Mahasu has not one but two Wazirs, one each for the Saathi and Pansi factions. The Wazir always comes from specific clans of the Rajput community. Pansi comes from the Rana clan and Saathi from the Panwar clan. Saathi Wazir looks after the affairs on the right bank of the Tons (i.e., of Bautha and Basik and Chalda when he is on their side). Pansi Wazir remains the minister of Pabsik and Chalda when he is on tour on that side. The ministers are responsible for managing the land held in the name of the king and his treasury which comprises the revenue from the land owned by Mahasu and the donations received by the temple.
4. ***Khund or Thani* (Warriors)**–They are the fearsome warriors from the Rajput community who accompany their king in his processions and guard the entourage from any obstacle or mishaps. They are short tempered and volatile, always ready to fight. The word khund is

derived from the word *khoon*, which, in the context, translates to being ready to shed their own blood as well as the blood of enemies. Each clan of khund has its cult centre (called Than in Rawain and Jaga in Mahasu realm), where they perform complicated rituals to their patron goddess, who is believed to bestow them with martial energy. Khunds of Chalda Mahasu are drawn from various areas of the Tons Valley to showcase their vast influence.

5. ***Bajgi* (Drummer Bards)**–In Hanol, the drummer bards are called bajgi, but those who get the privilege to perform at the temple of Hanol are called *deval*. They perform the dual function of musicians and the genealogists—the keeper of the collective memories of the community. They are tasked to sing the glories of Mahasu and their various exploits during public festivals. Through their complicated rhythmic drumming, they wake up the deity and create a charged, trance-like atmosphere during public gatherings.

In a nutshell, the deity pronounces his judgments through his oracle, while the rituals are performed by the priest. The priest is derived from a specific clan of Brahmins, while the oracle can be either Brahmin (Nautiyals in case of Karna) or Rajput (in case of Bautha Mahasu). The temple affairs are managed by Wazirs who are always from a specific Rajput clan—Rana, Panwar or Rawat. They are literate and aristocratic in their manner and attributes. In contrast, the khund or thani warriors are drawn primarily from clans who are considered 'rough and volatile'. Bajgi drummers belong to the bottom-most rung of society. This complex socio-political system is employed by the divine kings found throughout the Tons Valley. It has shown remarkable resilience and continues to be practised to present times.

The degree to which each caste plays a role in helping their divine king perform their kingship duties effectively is displayed during the ritual procession of the deity. Processions of local Gods is a regular feature of Pahadi culture. When a calamity befalls a village or social relations become strained, the village extends an invitation to the Mahasu to visit their village and remove any bad influences. They give a written application to the Wazir with a little silver as a tribute. The Wazir fixes the date after consulting with the God who gives his assent through his oracle.

On the appointed day, the God is woken up by Bajgi drummers through their ritual drumming. He is seated in a palanquin inside a silver box covered with a cloth. The *nishaan* (sign of the deity), is a silver tong with a coloured cloth wrapped around it, is carried by his followers. Others carry the parasol, cooking pots and other items belonging to the god. Rajput men carry the procession. It is led by Bajgi drummers and trumpeters who herald the king's arrival. The

Figure 38 The welcoming of the King's palanquin by villagers with local temple in the background

procession reaches the village and is placed at the designated platform. All villagers fast and break it only after the deity assumes his rightful place in the house of the village headman. Inviting and hosting the deity is a collective act. It is also an expensive affair. The whole village is mobilised and together bears the financial burden of making arrangements for hundreds of people accompanying the deity. But every person fulfils his role without complaining as hosting their divine king is an act of great honour and the merits of his blessings will be showered upon the whole village. The daily life of the Pahadi community revolves around doing their duties towards their divine kings, referred to simply as *Devta ka Kaam,* with a sincere heart. This duty engenders in them a sense of purpose and contributes towards maintaining the cosmic order.

Not only social, but the ritual processions have immense political significance in the Indian theory and application of kingship. For any king, territory is of prime consideration. Without a land to rule, there can be no king. As a king, Mahasu has sovereign rights over territory and population. His frequent palanquin processions are a way of defining and marking his royal territory. By journeying in his land, Mahasu renews his relations with his subjects who—through the collective act of hosting, inviting and feeding the God in their personal homes—reaffirm their allegiance to their divine king. The act of being invited and fed in the homes of subjects is an important test of kingship, for if the king is

Figure 39 A ritual procession at Kotgaon, Sankri

fed outside in public, it means he is treated as a guest, which is a subtle display by the public that they do not accept him as their king.

The allegiance of people is put to test during the procession of Chalda Mahasu, who is constantly on the move. His procession is a test of his subject's faith in him, who trek for miles in difficult terrain barefoot and lightly-clothed. The procession route is not defined and God, speaking through his oracle, can change the route suddenly or halt at a place for an indefinite period. The subjects follow their lord's directions without questioning them with the belief that the more difficulties they bear, the greater would be the merit accrued.

In 2009, Chalda Mahasu was on tour in the Pansi region of Himachal Pradesh. En route, he announced that he will halt for the first time in the small village of Shiraji. This hamlet had recently witnessed a turn in its fortune when it began practising apple farming. Chalda Mahasu arrived at the village and declared that a grand temple be built for him at this site. The villagers and his followers complied and it took five years for his shrine to be completed. This resulted in Chalda extending his stay on the Himachal side of the river from his usual 12 to 19 years. This extended stay led to whispers that the always mobile god has decided to become sedentary like his brothers. However, as soon as the temple was completed in Shiraji, Chalda announced that his procession would continue and, as per tradition, he would cross the river to visit the other side of his territory. The procession made steady progress and reached the old and dilapidated suspension bridge over river Tons. The public frenzy was at an all-time high as crossing the river was akin to crossing the boundary, and Chalda's visit to this side of the river had already been considerably delayed. The people of the Saathi side were eager to host their divine king. The district magistrate of Dehradun was directed by the Chief Secretary to make requisite arrangements to ensure the peaceful transition of Chalda Mahasu. Engineers of the Public Works Department studied the bridge and declared it unsafe for large crowds. Finally, a police force was deputed to ensure that no more than 20 people cross the bridge at a time. Meanwhile, the council of elders were busy planning to host and feed thousands of people accompanying the procession. But one major problem occurred. No one was sure about the date of the crossing. Only Mahasu could tell when he wished to cross, but his oracle was silent. The District Magistrate was restless, since the government machinery could not be deployed indefinitely. After the following day, winter season would begin as per the traditional calendar, and the Devta wouldn't be able to go out for the next 6 months. Seeing the delicate situation and the impatient crowd waiting to host their king, the Wazir of Pansi took off his cap and presented it before the oracle in a gesture of supplication and requested the God to make his move. Chalda possessed his mali and, through him, accused the Wazir of not wanting to keep the

Devta on his side. The request and negotiations continued, and the Devta eventually decided to cross. As of May 2023, retinue of Chalda Mahasu is stationed at the Dasau Pashgaon village.

To experience firsthand the institution of Mahasu kingship in the Tons Valley, a trip was organised by the author to Hanol the principal centre of Mahasu worship in February 2022. Located at a distance of a few kilometres from the temple at Hanol is Devbhoomi Homestays. Six cottages stand in a row amidst the towering mountains; outside, a small garden blooms with small yellow mustard flowers. Exhausted after hours of long travel from Dehradun and completely famished, we quickly dumped our luggage in our rooms and sat down to eat in the small but clean mess. Jeetu, the owner of the property, welcomed us warmly and quickly jotted down our order. He would move back and forth from the kitchen to the hall to convey the patrons' orders to his staff and bring the prepared food to the tables. He would always remove his slippers at the entrance, no matter how many times he was required to do so. When enquired about the reason behind this action, he announced with pride that he was one of the oracles of Mahasu Devta and, hence, was expected to follow a set of rules, one of which was to not enter the kitchen with footwear on. Elaborating further, he explained that oracles did not eat chicken or egg, and if they saw a dead cow or a

Figure 40 A family listening to the oracle in the courtyard of Mahasu temple, Hanol

dead human body, they skipped a meal and ate only after taking a bath.

The possession by the Devta is called *that*[55] Bautha and Pavasi Mahasus have many oracles, and Jeetu is one among them. After they possess him, he cannot remember anything. Basik Maharaj is more selective and prefers to speak through only one oracle. Chalda Mahasu has more than one, but fewer than his other siblings.

Thanking Jeetu for sharing his insights, we left for the temple of Hanol. It was a bright sunny day, and a giant board, enumerating the rules to be followed, greeted us at the entrance. After removing all the leather items from our purses, belts and phone covers, we washed our hands and entered the vast courtyard. A quaint structure, built in the local style and full of colourful wooden carvings, stood before us. On the raised platforms surrounding the temples sat a few local families. Dressed in traditional attire and sitting cross-legged, they watched with rapt attention to a man taking out rice grains and examining them before scattering them around him. Suddenly, the man started shivering. He threw a handful of rice in the air and began speaking in an agitated voice. The Devta had possessed him and was answering the questions of great personal importance to the family—prospects for the daughter's marriage, the timing of the birth of children, etc—diagnosing the cause of a misfortune, and suggesting the remedy to a *dosh* (harm) which had befallen the aggrieved family, just like it did the tehsildar.

Any disrespect to Mahasus invites their wrath and calamities (called dosh in local parlance) and continues to befall the offender until he apologises for his mistake through the proper rituals. The four brothers exhibit their offence and forgiveness in different ways, in accordance with their personalities. Bautha Mahasu has a share in every tribute offered by the aggrieved as a *dosh nivarana* (remedy) irrespective of the source of the misfortune. Basik Maharaj is very calm and generally does not take offence easily, but when it does happen, it destroys the entire family. Pabsik Mahasu gets angry very easily but is easy to please as well. The most difficult to handle is Chalda Mahasu; prickly by nature, he is easily offended and it takes strong efforts to please him.

One of the primary functions of a king is dispensing justice to his subjects, and the divine kings perform this function through their oracles. Traditionally, any disputes regarding competing claims on land were settled in the temple of Mahasu through a judicial method called the *loon lota* system. Under this method, the claimants would bring the soil or produce of their land to the temple. Both parties were required to swear an oath before the God. The oracle would take a lump of salt and start mixing it with water, proclaiming that the individual who has taken a false oath would dissolve in thin air, just as this salt is getting dissolved in water. The fear thus struck in the hearts of the false claimants would lead to the latter backing off and the dispute gets resolved. But when both parties pass the oath, the resolution moves to the next stage. Here, the possessed oracle would carefully examine the soil or produce from the field brought by each party, question the disputants and, after being satisfied with the answers, pronounce his judgement. This judicial process was so effective that the British did not establish any formal policing system here, leaving it to the courts of these divine kings to deal with the crimes in their own peculiar way. Today, the practice continues, and the functions of the police are performed by the tehsildar in absence of a formal policing system.

The absence of any written records before the arrival of the British who had a habit of recording everything, makes it difficult to reconstruct the history of the region. Traditionally, the past was preserved in the form of stories and songs by the Bajgi bards-drummers and although steeped in supernatural elements, their ability to faithfully preserve some facets of truth should not be ignored. The socio-politico-religious culture of Jaunsar-Bawar revolves around the Mahasu brothers and the lore sung by Bajgi drummers narrates their arrival from the magical land of Kashmir. This is corroborated by some evidence. The Mahasu brought with them some elements from Kashmir, chief among them being Naga worship and a knowledge of *tantra* (a diverse set of esoteric texts that emphasize rituals and techniques to achieve spiritual liberation and worldly success).

Naga worship has always been very popular in Kashmir. Kalhana's Rajatarangini is replete with references to Nagas, the earliest inhabitants of Kashmir since the time the valley was formed by draining of a primordial lake. Nagas were worshipped by Kashmiris as tutelary deities of numerous springs and lakes dotting the valley. The Mahasus have also been traditionally depicted as Nagas who emerged from the belly of four other Nagas and reside in a lake in the Kashmir valley when Una comes with his plea. Similarly, Kashmir was the major centre of Tantric scholarship[56] before Islamic invasions in fourteenth century. Sophisticated Tantric theories and modes of practices were developed by Kashmiri scholars. This influenced all major sects and religions leading to new schools of thought—Pratyabhijna or Kashmiri Shaivism and Pancaratra Vaishnavism. *Sanch Vidya* is one such Tantric text used by khund warriors in Jaunsar-Bawar for periodic ritual consecration of their cult centre, and by priests to make astrological predictions. The terms used for the system established by Mahasus are words derived from the Persian—mali, wazir, khund etc. The presence of Persian vocabulary in these remote regions which have never been under Islamic rule is surprising. However, Kashmir had come under Muslim rule by early fourteenth century in medieval period, which might have triggered the migration of Mahasu princes. Looking at these facts, it can be reasonably hypothesised that four princely brothers with Shaiva leanings hailing from Kashmir migrated to Jaunsar-Bawar with their small retinue during medieval times and brought with them certain cultural influences prevalent in Kashmir.

The region of Jaunsar-Bawar had historically remained on the periphery of Garhwal kingdom in the east and Sirmaur kingdom in the west. Spread of political control by human kings was checked by the presence of divinity acting as kings. Absence of any popular tirthas and poor availability of fertile land may have been a factor behind the low attention paid by the kings of neighbouring Garhwal and Sirmaur, to incorporate the region in their respective kingdoms. While the Puranas and epics praise the Ganga and other rivers of Garhwal and list the numerous benefits of bathing in their waters, river Tons, which derives its names from word *Tamasa*, was considered dark and polluted.

Indian philosophy talks about the three *gunas,* or qualities, of nature: *Sattva, Rajas* and *Tamas*. Tamas characterises impurity, laziness, darkness and ignorance. The river is said to be formed by the blood and tears of demons who, after being defeated by the Mahasus, escaped to the upper reaches of permanent snow. This negative connotation with the river manifested in the absence of bathing ghats and temples along its bank except the Mahasu ones.

The written history of the regions began with colonial rule when many British administrators and travellers started recording their observations and interactions in personal diaries, letters, official documents and gazetteers. After the Anglo-Gurkha War ended and the Treaty of Sagauli signed in March 1816, the Garhwal territories were divided between those under direct rule by British administrators and those that were indirectly ruled through local rulers as their representatives. Dehradun and Mussoorie were retained by the British and attached to the adjoined district of Saharanpur. For Jaunsar-Bawar, the British could not locate any direct claimants, as the region was under the divine rule of Mahasu. The British were equally fascinated and terrified by this region and its people. On the one hand, they were impressed by their war-like nature. They had begun to rise against the Gurkhas before the Anglo-Gurkha war and aided the British by cutting the supply lines of Gurkhas during the battles. But, on the other hand, the prevalence of unusual practices—the cult of the Mahasu, oracular possessions, animal sacrifices, headhunting and, most of all, fraternal polyandry—terrified them. As a result, they brought the region under their direct control by attaching it to the Dehradun district. Despite constituting one district, the two portions, Dun Valley and Jaunsar-Bawar, were governed under two different arrangements. While the system of magistrate/collector and regulations in force in other territories governed by East India Company were applicable to Dun Valley, Jaunsar-Bawar was made a scheduled district. A cantonment headquarters at Chakrata administered the entire region with the help of a small staff of patwaris, the revenue officials at village level who dealt with collection of taxes and maintainance of land records. Unlike their plains-counterparts, they performed all important functions related to revenue policing. Collection of land revenue was a very important matter for the East India Company and due attention was paid to land settlements, i.e., measurement of arable land and calculation of potential revenue, which were updated at periodic intervals. Although the limit to agricultural expansion is a problem common to mountains, this was more acute in the case of the Tons Valley. The colonial administrators noticed that,

> 'Even in the hills, Jaunsar-Bawar has the character of being one of the wildest and the most rugged tracts, affording naturally very little ground and that only in small patches. The mountains are peculiarly rough and precipitous, there is much cliff and rock and few villages so that the cultivation is necessarily small and very laborious.'[57]

Since no further expansion of agriculture was possible in these rugged hills, the practice of resettlement after every few years was stopped after 1874 when the administrators noticed the negligible economic growth in the previous 25 years. With an already limited revenue base, the British were extremely sensitive about any revenue not ending it their treasury. This brought them in conflict with Mahasu who also claimed to be the sovereign of the land. The ritual touring of the Mahasu was especially frowned upon by British administrators. Hosting and feeding the Mahasu procession with thousands of people in tow was a costly affair and all the expenses were borne by the villagers. Moreover, Mahasu also levied and collected *kut* (taxes) from his subjects, even though the British formally controlled the region. The frustration Mahasu caused among the British officials while dealing with the natives, who protested loudly over increase of tax by a single *anna* (lowest denomination of money used in Indian subcontinent. 1/16th of one rupee.) but spent happily while hosting Mahasu, is discernible in their memoires, letters and reports to one another. The longest reigning administrator of the Dehradun district (1815–1842), Major Young, who had played a pivotal role in the victory of the British against the Gurkhas, described in length the malignant influence of the Mahasu on the entire region of Jaunsar-Bawar. He noted that when the construction of the Chakrata-Tiuni-Shimla Road was in progress, the procession of Chalda Mahasu arrived. This distracted the workers so much that they remained absent for a long time.

Further, he notices that the God does not visit any village without an invitation, but the terror inspired by him was such that he was invited whenever a misfortune befell any village. In the 1827 report to Governor Metcalfe apprising him of updates on revenue collection, Young writes that all the *khats* (a revenue division comprising group of villages) had paid their dues on time except one, which had suffered from a landslide, causing damage to property. Mahasu Devta was invited and within a very short time on arrival, collected ₹588 besides the value of offerings the amount of which could not be ascertained[58] while the khat could pay revenue of only ₹2,000 to the collector. The British accused the Mahasu of spoiling the superstitious peasants so much with their exactions that the British administration was constantly deprived of revenue for which they had won the region with great difficulty. This prompted Major Young to intervene and try to put an end to the practice of the ritual touring of Mahasu. He called a meeting of all *sayanas* (headmen of a group of villages) in Kalsi, and in their presence, ordered the Wazir of Mahasu to stop accepting any more invitations henceforth. But the diktat was simply ignored by the locals. The British did not have sufficient local support and administrative machinery to enforce their decision by force. They tried to cope with this issue by misconstruing the problem and labelling the Mahasu exactions as a simple temple donation drive by locals.

After Independence, based on recommendations of a committee formed to study the extent of the backwardness of the region, the entire region, rather than a specific community, was granted the status of Scheduled Tribe through the gazette notification on 24 June 1967. With time, these, once inaccessible valleys of Tons and its tributaries, became connected to the outside world, along with the development of infrastructure and communication. Increase in contact has led to a sharp decline in the social customs of bride price, polyandry and animal sacrifices. Despite the influx of modern state machinery and instruments like the police and state systems, the significance of the Mahasu and other devtas remains. To this date, political leaders offer their prayers to seek the permission and blessings of Mahasu Devta before filing their nomination for an election. Many people still depend on the deity and his system of justice instead of approaching the police or the courts. Many youngsters from this region have migrated to other areas in search of better opportunities, just like other parts of the Uttarakhand state, but they make it a point to visit their villages whenever Chalda Mahasu is visiting or stopping in their village. Jubin Nautiyal, a famous playback singer, hails from Jaunsar-Bawar. He garnered recognition through singing a number of Bollywood hits, and did not hesitate to invoke the Mahasus' name and attribute his success to the blessings of these divine kings.

9

THARU & BOKSA: TRIBES OF TERAI

In 1815, the British won control of Kumaon, held by the Gurkhas since 1790 after the disposal of Chand dynasty, and acceded to the British through the peace treaty of Singrauli.[59] As per the treaty, river Kali was fixed as the boundary between the Company's territory and that of the Gurkhas from Nepal. To ensure the complete withdrawal of the Gurkhas from the region and to be prepared in case they decided to attack again, a large number of Company troops were deployed in Kumaon, in the areas of Champawat and Pithoragarh adjacent to Nepal.

Before the political control of East India Company, Kumaon was an agrarian society with a simple economic and social structure. The region was dotted with numerous self-sufficient and sparsely populated villages, isolated from each other by mountains. Even in Almora, the capital of Chand kings since 1560, the population barely reached to 4,000. The mountainous topography shaped the social and economic milieu of the region by putting limits on agricultural expansion. The villagers practised subsistence farming and the small surplus generated was traded with Bhotias, in exchange for salt and borax brought from Tibet. The simplicity of their lifestyle was also reflected in their social organisation. Social classes were few, especially in contrast to villages in the plains where complex hierarchies and specialised labour forces, divided into numerous *jatis* (classes) and *sub-jatis* (sub-classes) were a norm. But in Kumaon, even Brahmins were peasants who tilled their land. Another peculiar feature of Pahadi society was the absence of *Vaishya*, (trader class). This was due to a lack of urban centres and villages being engaged in a simple barter system for their needs.

In such a milieu, the sudden arrival of 15,000-20,000 British Company troops with their camp followers created problems. An immediate challenge before the Company was how to feed its soldiers. It tried to increase the amount of land that was under cultivation but met with limited success. The cultivated land could not be expanded much, owing to constraints put on by geography. Coupled with this, was the issue of transport. When the troops were on the move, they had to be supplied grains. But the absence of well-maintained roads made carriage of grains, equipment and luggage difficult. William Gardener, the first Commissioner of Kumaon, was responsible for civil administration, while the Company troops were under a military commander and separate from civil affairs. To manage the problem of grain supply and transportation, a haphazard *purwana* system was developed. Under this system, a purwana, or a written order of authorization, was issued by both civil and military officers to the village headman along with a fixed amount to be paid on the spot. The order mentioned the specific number of men required to act as *khuseea* (unpaid labour) for the transportation of men and luggage from one post to another; and the amount of grain expected to be delivered to the nearest military go-down within a given timeframe. Any failure to comply with the directives would result in fines or imprisonment or both. Unofficially, the troops simply seized grains from the villages and pressed whatever labour they could find to act as porters.

When William Traill became the Commissioner of Kumaon in 1818, he became aware of a simmering discontent among the locals. Through extensive tours, he developed an understanding of the region and its people, and tried to develop a functional market system called *khoosh khureed* where a voluntary exchange of grains for cash could take place. Sourcing the grains locally was much easier and cheaper than importing them from the plains. An added advantage would be that the income from the sale of grain could be used by peasants to meet the land tax imposed by the Company. However, the most significant reason was the aversion shown by hill men towards venturing into the plains. The route passed through a mysterious belt of dense forest which was dubbed by them as the Zone of Death. It was believed that death lurked among its thick foliage where even the sun failed to reach. Anyone who dared to cross the region, especially during the summer months, would be plagued by death and die within a few days.

To prevent the local discontent from turning into a law-and-order issue, Traill issued a series of orders in 1818 that prohibited the system of purwana and made the sale of grains by Pahadi peasants optional and voluntary. The most difficult task was to get the military officials to adapt to the new laws, accustomed as they were to the old system. Traill tried to achieve this by avoiding any direct confrontation with the army and resorting to persuasion by writing personal letters and communication. Thus, through his personal efforts and charismatic personality, Traill maintained a delicate balance between the civil and military administration and protected the peasants of Kumaon from the military's excesses. This, in turn, increased the confidence placed by locals in the new market system, ensuring an uninterrupted supply of grains to meet the needs of the army.

Traill retired in December 1835 and his successor, Colonel George Gowan, assumed charge in 1836. Gowan was, in many ways, the opposite of Traill, lacking an awareness of the region and persuasion skills of his predecessor. Within a few days of his posting, he got into a heated dispute with Colonel Andee, the Military Commander of Kumaon, straining his relations with the army. The influence of civil administration, thus, gradually waned, undoing all the progress Traill had made, and the army soon resumed the old practice of issuing purwanas and demanding grains from the villages. In 1837, a rumour spread in the countryside that a famine was about to befall the region. Panicked, the villages began hoarding their grain. The food supply to the markets of Almora and the British headquarters dropped sharply and no amount offered could induce the villagers—who firmly believed the rumour—to sell their produce to the army. Unfamiliar with local customs, Gowan did not understand that for most Kumaonis, the practice of selling grain was an alien concept and that they felt no obligation to supply it to anyone, especially when there was a looming crisis of potential shortage. He tried many things to solve this crisis. He ordered the police to search the town for hoarded grain, but it yielded little result. He ordered the tehsildar of Lohaghat to procure the grain at any cost, even if it necessitated the use of force. This also did not increase the supply of grain. Finally, by the middle of 1838, when the military was on the verge of starvation, Gowan decided to import the grains from the plains to the south. He wrote to the Commissioners of Bareilly and Moradabad, who promptly responded to his call. The path from the plains of Moradabad and Bareilly to the hills of Almora is where the forests with the aforementioned Zone of Death lay. In the absence of roads, the carts could not travel through the forest and, from here on, the khuseea were to carry the load on their backs for the rest of the journey. The thought of crossing the dreaded forest belt and carrying luggage through it was harrowing for all the coolies. But Gowan forced them to continue with the task. In the end, the fears of the porters proved true. A considerable number of them perished a few days into their journey in the Zone of Death.

Separating the Himalaya and the Ganges plains are two narrow belts—Bhabhar and Terai—running parallel to the mountain ranges. The first belt, Bhabar is a waterless tract which starts from the base where the mountain's slopes end and runs until Terai to its south. Numerous small streams originate in the Middle Himalaya and travel shorter distances before leaving the mountains. On their way, they erode and carry big boulders, stones and gravel which they deposit at the base of the hills they exit. With the passage of time, this huge mass brought by the river spread out to form a gently sloping tract running 16-24 kilometres away from the base of the mountains. The seasonal streams disappear here, while the larger rivers of Gaula and Kosi show a reduction in their volume. This happens because the water is absorbed by the

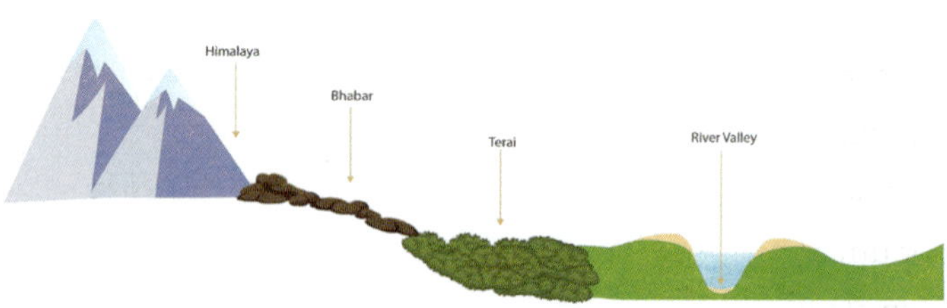

Figure 41 The geography of Bhabhar-Terai

porous gravelly bed but is retained by an impervious bed present below the gravelly layer. Bhabar is a densely forested region where *sal* and *haldu* trees are found aplenty. The Bhabar belt is well-developed in a region bounded by the Ramganga river to the west to the Sharda/Kali river to the east.

Running south of Bhabar is the Terai belt, over 19 kilometres wide. The streams which had disappeared in Bhabar reappear here. The presence of numerous springs along its northern boundary indicates the starting of Terai, while its southern boundary merges with the Gangetic plains. The sudden reappearance of so much water makes Terai swampy, turning it essentially into a grassland, full of tall, elephant grass mixed with forests. The belts of Bhabar-Terai are insignificant in Garhwal, where the presence of the Shivaliks prevents the development of these two separate belts and instead, forms an elevated Dun Valley with mixed characteristics of both the belts. The presence of the much longer and bigger rivers of Yamuna and Ganga is another reason for their insignificance. These fast-flowing rivers originate from the glaciers of the greater Himalaya and carry huge volumes of water throughout the year. They deposit their gravel, boulders and shingles in their upper reaches, bringing only finely eroded silt to the plains.

The title of the Zone of Death earned by Terai-Bhabar is not unfounded. A dangerous place, untamed and wild, where even elephants could move undetected in the tall grasses, there was always the possibility of coming face-to-face with wild animals. In its density, where even sunlight could not reach, ferocious bandits found safety and refuge and would often kill any passer-by. As a result, navigating this zone always held the danger of losing both life and property. Still, during winters, the hill shepherds moved to the borders of Terai to graze their livestock and trade with *deshis* (the plains people). However, it was during the wet summer months, from April to November, that this region was altogether avoided. During the rainy season, when streams overflowed and the marshy area became more waterlogged, the circumstances created an ideal breeding ground for malarial mosquitos. The malarial fever was a deadly disease which, once contracted, often ended in death and, if a person survived, would cause serious deformities for the rest of his life. Half of the porters who picked up the load in Bhabar-Terai in this unhealthy season contracted the disease and ten percent of them lost their lives.[60] Despite presenting extreme adverse conditions, the place was not entirely devoid of human habitation. The tribes of Tharu and Boksa entered this region in the medieval period and made it their home, regardless of the challenges thrown by geography.

Both Tharu and Boksa have the same ethnic origin, at least according to folklore, although Boksas are considered offshoots of Tharu by anthropologists. The oral history of the Tharus puts them as descendants of soldiers who fought valiantly by the side of Maharana Pratap, the sixteenth century king from Rajasthan famous for his lifelong resistance against the Mughal rule. The Boksas also claim descent from King Jagatdeo, a ruler from Rajasthan. The common element in their oral history is that to save themselves from the Mughal persecution, these warriors sought refuge in the dense forests of the Terai. In some versions, it was the royal ladies who took shelter in Terai to save their honour and subsequently settled there. Hence, both tribes consider themselves Rajputs.

Chiefly dependent on the forests for their sustenance, the population practised small-scale shifting agriculture, where they cleared a small patch of trees and moved on to a new clearing after harvesting their crops. The geography was not suitable for cultivation, but the forests were full of wildlife; hence, to supplement their diet, they lived off the meat of whatever animal they could hunt, sometimes even carrying off the leftovers of prey killed and partially eaten by tigers. Fishing was another mode of supplementing their diet, while home-brewed liquor made the existence among the dangerous surroundings less worrying. This fondness for fish and liquor, prevalent among the Tharus and Boksas, was also noticed by British administrators.

A unique social custom called *kanya shulk* (bride price) exists among these tribes. While in mainstream societies, the bride's family has to pay dowry upon her marriage, here, the reverse happens. It is customary for the groom to pay money, called *malgati*, to the bride's family. Sociologists think the reason behind this custom is that because women play an important role in economic activities ranging from working on fields, gathering fuel and fodder and looking after households, her family loses her contribution after her marriage. This loss is compensated by malgati. The bride price is one of the main reasons for fewer divorces in the tribe, though it is not prohibited. Divorced or widowed women easily get new husbands, but the same is not the case for men because of an adverse sex ratio and the compulsory bride price. If a woman leaves her husband, however, then her father has to return her malgati to her former husband. If a woman leaves her husband and remarries, then the new husband has to pay the bride price, to the previous husband.

The culture of this tribe has been portrayed in a short story titled *Pre-Red Tape Days* by Jim Corbett, a renowned hunter and astute observer of local culture. Based on his close study of the Boksa tribe, he found two primary traits which made them stand out, one being their impeccable cleanliness. He found the village, as well as individual houses of the Boksas clean and well maintained in comparison to other places. The other peculiar feature was the superior position enjoyed by the Boksa women, which was absent in Indian society during colonial period. Although the same was true with Tharus also, this practice has been well documented by the British in the case of Boksas.

Corbett describes a cold winter morning in the 1930s, when he and his friend, the superintendent of Terai and

Bhabar division Frederick Anderson, were on tour of a Boksa village as part of Anderson's magisterial duty. Anderson was hearing and settling petitions brought to him by the people of Boksa village. The entire population had assembled at a spot, just outside the village. Anderson listened to a petition by a complainant named Chadi who had accused another villager, Kalu, of abducting his wife, Tilni. When called to defend himself, Kalu claimed that Tilni had come to him of her own free will. The audience, especially the women-folk who had shown little interest in previous cases, was now listening in rapt attention. Tilni was also present in the crowd and when she was called, a young attractive girl presented herself before the court. When Anderson asked why she had left Chadi, she responded fearlessly that she had willingly moved in with Kalu, as her husband was not only dirty but also a miser. Despite being married for two years, he had failed to provide for her needs. In fact, the clothes she was wearing, the silver bangles adorning her wrists and the strings of glass beads around her neck were all gifts from Kalu. No matter the amount of pressure applied by the court, she would not go back to her husband. This was most unusual, for no woman elsewhere in India would have dared to plead her case so openly before a crowd, especially announcing her decision to leave her husband and stay with another man.

An adamant Chadi put his foot down and demanded ₹150 as compensation from Kalu. The man wished to negotiate and offered to pay ₹50 as compensation. He further argued that Chadi had married Tilni for ₹100, and then she was a virgin. A heated debate, held in whispers, erupted amongst the audience. It was finally decided that Kalu would pay ₹75 to Chadi, which he paid after collecting the balance amount from his friends among the audience. Before Anderson could dismiss the case, a woman with a deformed body appeared before the audience. Her face was full of sorrow and her gait limped, for she had suffered immensely from malaria, the scourge of Terai, which had left her permanently deformed. She stood before Anderson with folded hands and asked in a tired voice, "What about me, Sir? I am Kalu's wife. Now that Kalu has got another wife, I would be rendered homeless. I have no relatives left and am too ill to find any work. I would die of illness and starvation." The woman started sobbing uncontrollably, adding to the audience's dilemma. Tilni consoled the woman, offering to take care of her and assured her that she would not have to move out of her home. But the final twist was yet to come. Chadi approached Anderson and requested to rescind his petition. He tore the paper into pieces and told Anderson that since Kalu has two mouths to feed now, of which one requires special care, he would not take any compensation. Saying this, Chadi handed the money back to Kalu and the case was declared settled by Anderson.

Both the tribes are found in the foothills of Garhwal as well as Kumaon Himalaya. Having lived in the swampy land for centuries, they have gradually developed some immunity from malaria. In Garhwal, they are found in the Vikasnagar and Doiwala blocks of Dehradun; in Kumaon, they are spread across the Ramanagar, Bajpur and Khatima blocks of Nainital and Udham Singh Nagar district. Khatima is chiefly a Tharu town. Their religious beliefs are identical to mainstream Hinduism and they worship the major deities of Hinduism. Holi is celebrated with great zeal. Since Tharus and Boksas have both lived in the same environment of Terai for centuries, they share similar cultural values. However, it is to be noted that there are no intermarriages between the tribes. In fact, there is no marriage even within the same tribes residing in different places. For instance, a Boksa of Vikasnagar would not marry a Boksa living in Haridwar, citing differences in their customs and traditions. In the past, Boksas were stereotyped by the people as practitioners of black magic. It was believed that a Boksa could transform himself into a tiger and carry off its unsuspecting victim, chiefly women, into the jungles to steal their jewellery and other valuables. This fear and suspicion made the Pahadi society to avoid any contact with these tribes so they lived in isolation for centuries until 1856, when Sir Henry Ramsay became the new Commissioner of Kumaon and transformed the region.

Not much attention was paid by the early Commissioners of Kumaon, to make the Terai-Bhabhar belt more productive, and this region was dismissed as a wasteland full of untamed wilderness. A great deal of Commissioner Traill's focus had been directed towards engaging in paper wars with the British authorities of Moradabad and Bareilly over the overlapping jurisdiction of Bhabar-Terai as its boundaries kept shifting, until the region was put under the control of the Kumaon Commissionerate. Traill introduced a grazing tax on shepherds grazing their cattle in Terai during the cool season. In 1834, Haldwani, a small trade mart equipped with temporary grass huts, was established for these hill shepherds carrying out seasonal small-scale trade. Traill considered the idea of bringing agriculture to Bhabar-Terai impossible owing to practical difficulties of its geography where water sinks and reappears in Terai, only to end in swamps. But Traill was ultimately proven wrong. Today, Haldwani is the largest city in Kumaon and the administrative head of the whole Kumaon. The city is notably surrounded by fields where agriculture is practised throughout the year.

The credit for the transformation of the Bhabar-Terai belt from a dangerous and barely populated place to an agriculturally prosperous and habitable township goes largely to Captain Henry Ramsay, the longest reigning Commissioner of Kumaon who held that post for 36 years. The British occupation of Kumaon and of India at large was based primarily on economic interests. While taxes on land was one of the major sources of income for the Company, the mountains of Kumaon provided limited scope for the expansion of agriculture. Hence, the British looked to the south, at the marshy, forested land of Bhabar-Terai, which suffered from problems of its own, foremost being geography unsuitable for irrigation. The challenges before Ramsay were enormous. But the then Lieutenant Governor of North-Western Provinces of India, James Thompson, had faith in Ramsay's capability. He put the region directly under Ramsay's charge and extended a permanent advance of ₹10,000, along with the freedom to improve the region as he deemed fit.

The first step taken by Ramsay was clearing the forest of dacoits and bandits who used it as retreat and shelter. This task was successfully executed by two officials, Fleetwood Williams and Moberly. Unfortunately, the latter lost his life from jungle fever while executing his duties. Ramsay also invested in building canals to not only bring the land under irrigation but also manage incoming water from the rivers Kosi and Gaula such that it was directed away from swamps and used for irrigating crops as per need and necessity. He and his team worked out detailed plans to maximise the number of *guls* (distributary channels) created off the principal rivers of Gaula and Kosi, with the least amount of water wasted. The water was regulated by sluice gates placed at the head of each channel which were opened and shut according to a fixed plan based on the extent of cultivation and nature of crop to prevent overflooding. The combined length of the canals constructed under Ramsay measured over 112 kilometres. The Ramanagar and Golawar canals were the most significant, the latter being the largest canal (at just over 90 kilometres) of its time and irrigating a cultivated area of 20,000 acres. Thus, the water which had earlier drained into swamps, allowing mosquitoes to breed, was now being diverted into these newly constructed canals.

At first, Ramsay tried to work with the Tharu and Boksa tribes to change their customary practice of shifting agriculture, which involved moving from one place to another. Instead, he wanted them to take advantage of the newly built irrigation facilities by settling down in one place and focusing their energy on improving new fields. However, the tribes simply continued with their water-inefficient practices. Witnessing their inability to judiciously manage resources, Ramsay turned his hopes towards the cultivators of the Kumaon mountains. He introduced lucrative revenue policies to encourage the locals to set up permanent villages in Terai-Bhabar. These newly settled villages need not pay any revenue for the first two years of settlement and the maximum revenue to be collected from these villages was kept low at 8 *annas* per *bigha,* or three rupees per acre. Earlier, people would avoid the belt during monsoon months, but encouraged by the government's policies and access to irrigation, peasants from the hills began settling permanently here and growing rice crops during the Kharif season. The fertile soil of Bhabar supported the production of rice, wheat, rapeseed and sugarcane crops which were in high demand. Another sector which saw enormous improvement under

Ramsay's reign was connectivity. Ramsay recognized that without good roads, the transport of goods and troops from the plains to the hills would always be fraught with difficulties. New cart roads were constructed joining important cities on the belt like Haldwani and Ramnagar, with headquarters at Almora and Nainital. New suspension and wire rope bridges were constructed over the principal rivers.

The success of Ramsay's tenure in transforming the Terai-Bhabar belt can be gauzed from the fact that 'revenue increased sixteen times the amount at which it was fixed when he undertook the charge, i.e., for each anna invested the government now gets a rupee.'[61] The major factor in this turnaround was the extension of irrigation facilities. This was noted by the British civil servant Edward T. Atkinson. Atkinson was an officer who first edited the multi-volume *Statistical, Descriptive and Historical Account of the North-Western Provinces of India* and, thereafter, got familiar with the North-Western Provinces (areas of present-day Uttar Pradesh) as a census official. He was tasked with producing many manuals and reports and the *Himalayan Districts* (reprinted as *Himalayan Gazetteer*) was one such project where he collected information about Himalayan districts, detailing their people, customs and revenue systems amongst other aspects. Atkinson notes in his Gazetteer, 'The prosperity of the Bhabar cultivation depends on irrigation and manure.'[62] The latter was obtained from cattle, which were available in plenty. But it was the problem of irrigation caused by hostile geography that Ramsay's intervention solved. The speed and scale of the transformation of Terai-Bhabar under Ramsay's administration was truly remarkable. New villages were found all over the tract by the hardy men brought down by Ramsay from the higher reaches of the Himalaya who, through their hard labour, had tamed the wilderness and brought the land under intense cultivation.

But one barrier still threatened to undo all the hard work done by Ramsay and the newly settled peasants. This challenge was malaria, locally known as Bhabar Fever. Jim Corbett recounts the sad tale of the once flourishing village of *Naya Gaon* (new village) established by Ramsay, whose inhabitants died from malaria; those left found employment elsewhere, putting an end to Naya Gaon. The fields carved out from the wilderness which used to yield bumper produce fell into disuse and the area reverted to being a jungle. Years later, an intrepid doctor from Punjab tried to re-establish the village, but when 'his daughter, wife and finally he himself died of malaria, Naya Gaon, for the second time, went back to the jungle.'[63] The disease continued to wreak havoc until better medical facilities and greater control over breeding grounds was exercised by the newly formed government of independent India in collaboration with the World Health Organisation (WHO).

With the last barrier to settlement removed, the region was rapidly settled by people coming from the hills, the plains and refugees from Pakistan, such that today, Haldwani is the administrative centre and also the largest city of Kumaon. Every inch of land was brought under plough and food production, soared exponentially. However, the development did not bode well for the Tharus and the Boksas, who became increasingly marginalised from their own land due to their illiteracy. In the absence of any written record of ownership, they were forced to work as bonded labourers on their own land. Their situation has showed gradual improvement after their inclusion in the list of Scheduled Tribes, a reserved category of marginalised people.

PART C

HIMALAYA: THE SHADES OF NATURE

10

BUGYALS: THE ENCHANTING MEADOWS

In his description about the many magical places of the Himalaya, Garuda told Galava, 'In the Himalaya, one can find many plains carpeted with grass. It is here that the most beautiful gardens of Kubera—Chitratha and Saugandhikanaka—lie, always guarded by fearsome *rakshasas* (demons). It was here that Kubera was installed as the emperor of Rakshasas, Yakshas and Gandharvas.'[64]

These majestic gardens of Kubera hosted some of the most dazzling flowers. One major episode of the *Mahabharata* took place in these gardens. This is when the Pandavas were staying in Badrinath, awaiting Arjuna's return from heaven. One day, a cool breeze brought with it a golden-hued lotus and dropped it in their hermitage. Draupadi was entranced by this beautiful lotus and its mesmerising fragrance. She requested Bhima to bring more, one for each of his brothers. Following the direction of the breeze, Bhima climbed the mountain Gandhamadana and travelled a long distance. He reached a forest and blew his conch to scare away the wild animals. Unknown to him, Lord Hanuman was sleeping in a nearby grove. The shrill blast of the conch disturbed him; in response, he struck his tail hard on the ground, the sound echoing in the forest. Alarmed, Bhima cautiously looked around for the source of the sound. He found Hanuman deep in his sleep and obstructing his way. Bhima, unable to recognize him, ordered him to move his tail and clear the way. Hanuman asked Bhima to move the tail himself. Despite all his might, Bhima failed to budge the tail by even an inch. He realised that this was no ordinary monkey and requested him to reveal his identity. Hanuman introduced himself and Bhima was delighted to meet his elder brother. Both are *Pavan putra* (sons of the wind god). After a philosophical question-answer session, Hanuman told him that the flower came from the Saugandhikanaka garden of Kubera and guided him to its location.

On his way, Bhima saw forests full of blossoms, with deer watching him as they grazed on the grass. He saw a wide river with colourful lotuses floating on its surface. At last, he saw a pond full of golden lotuses, situated in an heavenly grove. It was the pleasure garden of Kubera, the Lord of the Yakshas. Fearsome Krodhavasas, a class of Rakshasas bearing clubs and weapons, were guarding its entrance. When Bhima approached, they stopped him, "No person, who is subject to the laws of the mortal world, can sport in this heavenly garden frequented by Gandharvas, Apsaras and hordes of other godly beings," Bhima replied fearlessly, saying that

Figure 42 Bhima reaching for the flower in Kubera's garden while surrounded by demon guards

this pond had been created by mountain springs, not by Kubera himself. Hence, their Lord did not possess the right to prevent anyone's entry. Saying this, he plunged into the pond and beat all the Rakshasas when they tried to stop him. Yudhishthira's arrival put an end to the battle and Kubera granted them the permission to stay in his pleasure garden.

On a cold misty morning in July 1931, a small party of six British mountaineers was returning from their expedition at Mount Kamet, one of the tallest peaks in the Garhwal Himalaya. Monsoon had arrived, and it was raining heavily. The party, miserable from the cold and obscured vision due to dense clouds, crossed the difficult Bhyundar Pass at the height of 5,000 metres. As they descended into a new valley of which they knew little, a patch of blue caught the eye of R.L Holdsworth, a member of the group who happened to be a botanist. With their descent, the clouds gradually dissipated, and the party found themselves in a place packed with so many flowers that it was impossible to walk without stepping on them. So enchanted was one member, Frank Smythe, by the view, that he again returned to the valley in 1937 and remained there for the entire monsoon period to collect and catalogue the seeds of different floral species. Locally called Bhyunder, Smythe referred the upper reaches of this narrow valley as the Valley of Flowers. He would go on to write a book with the same title, *The Valley of Flowers,*

Figure 43 Way to Valley of Flowers

in 1938 which introduced the outside world to the beauties of this land. In 1982, to better protect the floral biodiversity the area, 125.6 square kilometres of the valley was given the status of National Park. In 2000, it was made part of adjoining Nanda Devi Biosphere Reserve and became the second core zone of the reserve with a rich concentration of endemic & rare floral species. This also prompted an inclusion in United Nations Educational, Scientific and Cultural Organization's (UNESCO) list of World Heritage Sites in 2005.

Could the Valley of Flowers with the rich concentration of rare floral species be in some way connected with the supernatural Saugandhikanaka garden of Kubera described in *Mahabharata*? Local folklore does certainly point to the association. As per the local lore, the valley was created by showering of flowers by the Gods from heaven to Earth, in celebration of the cosmic events which occurred in its neighbourhood. The flower-filled valley then became *Nandan Kanan* (celestial garden) of Indra where supernatural beings, especially Apsaras, the gorgeous nymphs of heaven, frequently sport in the waters and collect flowers with their friends. Any unsuspecting male who ventures late in the night is taken by the Apsaras to the world beyond. The valley is also drained by a river called *Pushpawati* (bearing of flowers). The name was given by the Pandavas when they visited this place and saw flowers floating on it.

KUBERA: THE LOCAL DEITY

Kubera, The Lord of Yakshas and Wealth, is worshipped in the region surrounding Valley of Flowers. At Badrinath, Kubera is worshipped as the treasurer to the deity, and his *murti* (statue) is brought to stay at the winter seat of Pandukeshwar every year. This is 2.5 kilometres from Govindghat, where the trek to the Valley of Flowers starts, and 10 kilometres from Hanumanchatti, the place where Bhima is believed to have met his brother Hanuman on his quest to get the flowers. North of Badrinath is the village of Mana, the last village on the border with China, inhabited by Bhotias. The word Mana, comes from Manibhadra, another name of Kubera, while a place named after the mythical city of Kubera, Alkapuri is also located at some distance from the village.

The trek to Valley of Flowers starts from Govindghat, 20 kilometres north of Joshimath. Trekking 10 kilometres from Govindghat and crossing cascading waterfalls and springs, one reaches Ghangaria where river Pushpawati coming from the Valley of Flowers meets Lakshman Ganga to form the Bhyunder river. Lakshman Ganga originates from Hemkund or Lokpal Lake located 6 kilometres upstream at a height of 4,329 metres. The sparkling blue lake is surrounded

Figure 44 Brahma Kamal

Figure 45 Inside a Brahma Kamal

by seven snow-covered mountains called the Saptrishi peaks, which also feed the lake through glacial melt. Growing on the rocky shores of the lake are the golden coloured lotuses called *Brahma Kamal*, literally, God's Lotus. Belonging to genera Saussera, the Brahma Kamal is the state flower of Uttarakhand. Golden-hued, it blooms for a very short time, and those who are able to witness this event are considered extremely lucky. Generally found in high meadows like the Valley of Flowers, it can also be seen growing on the rocky slopes and shores of alpine lakes like Roopkund and

Hemkund. The flower is said to possess a strong fragrance which might be overwhelming for some people. To survive in an environment full of strong winds, freezing cold and prolonged snowfall, these flowers have developed certain adaptive features. The purple-coloured flowers are bound together in a tight bunch and are wholly covered by golden papery brackets which protect the delicate flowers from the harsh environment that surrounds them.

The gently rolling meadows carpeted with herbaceous grasses and found in the higher ranges of the Himalaya are called Bugyals. The term Bugyal has been derived from Bug or Bugi, a collective term in Uttarakhand for several dwarf grasses such as, Dudh Bug (*Euphoria Stracheyi*), Dhania Bug (*Trachydium Roylei*), Bus Bug (*Saussurea Graminifolia*), and Mamla Bug (*Kobresia*) species which grow in great profusion in these meadows.[65] The Bugyals are found between an altitude of 3,600 to 4,500 metres where the treeline ends, continuing until the snowline. They remain under snow for the most part of the year, and during the short monsoon months of July, August and September, the meadows become a carpet of lush green grass filled with myriad wildflowers. In Uttarakhand, around 24% of the geographical area falls within the alpine zone and hosts these beautiful and sundry meadows. Around 75-80 of such Bugyals, ranging from a few to 400 square kilometres in area, are spread across the

Figure 46 The meadows between the treeline and snowline

state in the upper reaches of its 14 major river valleys. Some of the most extensive Bugyals with richest biodiversity are located around basins of Nanda Devi, Kedarnath, Gangotri and Bandarpoonch area of the Greater Himalaya. Many of these are popular trekking destinations today, frequented by the youth and enthusiasts every year. Around 400 Medicinal & Aromatic Plant (MAP) species have been reported in the Bugyals, many being endemic to the region, making Bugyals one of the chief biodiversity hotspots of the state.

The meadows are not only rich in floral diversity but host many endemic faunal and avifaunal species as well. In fact, the state animal of Uttarakhand, the musk deer, and the state bird, the multicoloured Himalayan monal, are abundantly found in these regions. As part of the fauna, 52 species of mammals have been catalogued, including the endangered

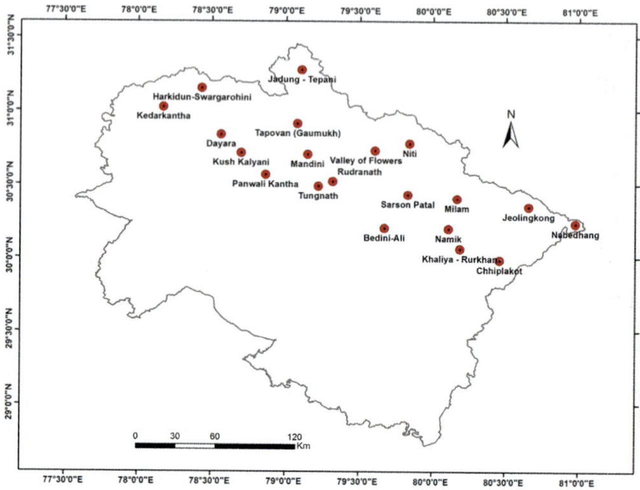

Figure 47 Distirbution of prominent Bugyals in Uttarakhand which are also popular pilgrimage and trekking sites

snow leopard, the Himalayan brown bear, the Himalayan marmot and a variety of ungulates (class of large herbivores with hoofs) like musk deer, bharal (blue sheep), hangul (Kashmir stag), etc. Similarly, among birds, the Bugyals are home to the Himalayan snowcock, golden eagle, snow pigeon and chukar partridge, among others.

The war between the armies of Rama and Ravana in Lanka showed no signs of concluding. There was commotion all around. Screams of pain and calls for help filled the air. With great difficulty, Hanuman succeeded in bringing the *Vanar* army to order after the chaos unleashed by the illusory tactics of Indrajeet, son of Ravana. Two days prior, Lakshman had killed Atikaya, another of Ravana's sons. Since then, retaliation from Indrajeet had been extremely harsh. Flying on his airborne chariot, he made himself invisible and shot numerous missiles, causing panic in Rama's army. Absent-mindedly, Hanuman rubbed the wound on his arm, stinging from the arrow that had grazed it. But Hanuman did not care for pain. He stared anxiously at the ground where his beloved Lord Rama and his brother, Lakshman, lay unconscious. They had tried to intervene but, unable to see Indrajeet, they had failed to counter the mighty Brahmastra missile hurled at them. Badly injuring the majority of the Vanars in Rama's army, Indrajeet had returned victorious, assuming the princes to be dead.

Although their breath hadn't left them, the princes' death was certain if nothing was done right away. Hanuman's chain of thought was broken by a voice calling for him. It was Jambavan, the wise old bear of the Vanar army. Laying injured, he addressed Hanuman, "O Pavana putra, you are blessed with mighty powers and you alone bear the capability to cross the ocean. Do make haste. Travel quickly to the Greater Himalaya, the foremost of all the mountains and full of wonders of Earth. Near the sacred peak of Mount Kailash lies a mountain called Dronagiri full of blazing herbs which glow in the dark. There, you will find four principal herbs—*Mrita Sanjeevani* (capable of restoring the dead to life), *Vishalyakarani* (capable of extracting weapons and healing all wounds inflicted by weapons), *Suvarnakarani* (restoring the body to its original complexion) and *Sandhani* (capable of joining severed limbs or mending fractured bone). Fetch these miraculous herbs with their supreme healing properties and save the dying princes along with the wounded Vanar army."[66]

Hanuman immediately set to work. Assuming a gigantic form, he leapt across the ocean and flew towards the great mountain ranges to the north. After hours of travel, he reached the snowy peaks of the Himalaya that were studded with clear streams, waterfalls, caverns and great hermitages where pious sages were engaged in austerities. Finally, he located the mountain which stood tall and glowing with the combined light of fluorescent herbs growing on its steep slopes. Sensing that someone was coming in search of them, the herbs stopped emitting light and disappeared from Hanuman's view. Angry, he addressed the mountain, "O mountain! Don't you have compassion for the injured prince of Ayodhya and the multitude of beings currently in extreme distress? If not, then face the strength of my arms today and find your pride shattered." Saying this, Hanuman uprooted the mountain and flew with great speed towards Lanka. Seeing Hanuman approaching with the mountain, a wave of joy spread in the Vanar army. Inhaling the fragrance of the miraculous herbs, Rama and Lakshman woke up from their slumber and regained their lost strength. When all the Vanar army had recovered from their wounds, Hanuman quickly carried the mountain of herbs back to its original place and joined the war against Ravana.

The mountain of Dronagiri mentioned in Ramayana is today identified with Mount Dunagiri, located in the Chamoli district and surrounded by the enchanting Bugyals of Nandikund and Sarson Patal. At the base of the mountain is a village called Dunagiri. There, a local version of the Ramayana is prevalent, according to which Hanuman worship is prohibited. As per this version, when Hanuman reached the place, he was unable to recognize the correct herb. Time was ticking by and he had to hurry. He looked for help and found an old woman awake in the village. Out of compassion, she pointed him to the correct mountain and Hanuman, in one swoop, sliced off a portion and flew away. The next morning, when the villagers awoke, they saw their beloved mountain defaced and bleeding from the wound. They were extremely angry and banished the woman who had helped Hanuman. To this day, the Ramlila performed in these villages do not mention Hanuman. This hillside is referred to as *Dev Parbat*. As part of the celebrations of a local festival called Jagar, in addition to the usual singing and dancing, the crowd also becomes possessed with the spirits of different local deities. When the spirit of the Dunagiri mountain deity possesses the body of a villager, one arm of the possessed person becomes limp and hangs lifeless, representing the damage done to the mountain by Hanuman by uprooting a part of it and taking it away to Lanka.

With the identification of the location of the mountain where the herb was said to be taken from, the next step in the minds of researchers and enthusiasts was to identify the herbs mentioned in Valmiki's Ramayana. Despite the mention of four principal herbs, it was the Mrita Sanjeevani—the herb capable of bringing the dead back to life—that captured the imagination of the public. The interest in its discovery received impetus after the formation of the separate state of Uttarakhand in 2000. The successive governments of the state and private organisations made efforts to identify the *sanjeevani booti*, as it came to be known. In 2008, Acharya Balkrishna of Patanjali Vidyapeeth surveyed these meadows and considered *Phen Kamal* (Saussurea gossypiphora) to be a potential candidate for the sanjeevani. This plant's tiny flowers are grouped in tight bunches and are embedded in woolly hair-like coverings which emit a faint glow at night—one of the characteristics of sanjeevani as told to Hanuman by Jambavan. Some have identified the sanjeevani herb as Selaginella bryopteris, which has shown many medicinal

Figure 48 Phenkamal flower

properties[67]. Still, no clear consensus has emerged on its identification. It is noteworthy that the Ramayana mentions not only sanjeevani, but also other medicinal herbs like *vishalya karani, suvarna karni* and *sandhani*. These are just a few of the rare medicinal herbs spread across these vast meadows which are not found anywhere else. Although their therapeutic properties have not been clinically established, they find extensive mention in Ayurveda—traditional Hindu medicinal system—and *Aanchi*—traditional Tibetan medicinal system used by local Bhotia communities. Various parts of these herbs, like rhizomes, flowers and leaves, are boiled and the extracted juice and oil converted into nutritious tonic and potions capable of providing relief from multiple ailments. For instance, the woolly hair of Phena Kamal is used as a bandage to stop bleeding. The Bugyal region of the state is said to host 300-400 plant species, out of which 50 are heavily used by locals. Many of these plants and herbs have started being commercially exploited for their medicinal properties. Currently in India, the pharmaceutical sector is using about 280 species of Medicinal and Aromatic Plants (MAPs), of which 175 species belong to the Himalayan ecosystem[68].

Keeda Jadi: The Himalayan Gold

Nicknamed as the 'Himalayan Gold', the Cordyceps or caterpillar fungus, locally called *Keeda Jadi* is found in the alpine meadows of the Himalaya. True to its name, this unique herb is formed when a parasitic fungus penetrates and inhabits the body of a caterpillar belonging to the moth species. The herb not only has a golden appearance, it fetches a price higher than gold—rupees 10 lakhs for a kilogram—in the international black market. The real reason behind the high demand is the purported medicinal benefits it bestows upon its users, especially as an effective cure for impotence. Long considered in the Chinese medicinal system to be an energy booster and an effective treatment for liver-related problems, the world took notice of Keeda Jadi in 1993 when many world records were broken by women Chinese athletes in 1500 metres, 3000 metres and 10000 metres track events. The shattering of five world records in a single event surprised everyone; the athletes' dope tests had turned out negative too.[69] It was later revealed that regular consumption of a Cordyceps-based diet was the reason behind the spectacular performance. Earlier, the demand for the herb remained focused in the mountains of Tibet, Bhutan and Nepal, but after a notable decline in the availability of the product in these regions, smugglers shifted their operations to Uttarakhand.

In Uttarakhand, Cordyceps is found in the meadows at a height of about 3500-4800 metres in Chamoli and Pithoragarh districts. Local families who do not have any other source of employment besides small-scale farming and tourism agree to search for the herb at these high altitudes. Every year, over 10,000 people—men, women and kids—throng these meadows and camp there for extended periods in the months of May and June, when the snow melts away and this insect herb becomes exposed. As everyone is engaged in the search, many take to venturing higher and higher where the climatic conditions are unsuitable for human presence. Here, the risk of fainting from low oxygen levels, contracting skin diseases from high UV exposure and chances of slipping to one's death while walking on snow-covered terrain is dangerously high. But the benefit that the trade of Keeda Jadi showers on the local community makes up for the dangers. Requiring neither educational qualifications nor any capital investment, the collection of around 150-300 pieces puts an income of around ₹1-3 lakhs per season in the hands of families which had been sustaining themselves on meagre income from agriculture.[70] A study of villages in Gori Ganga Valley revealed that the income from Keeda Jadi collection[71] contributes to 60-78% of annual household earnings. This has motivated people from adjoining districts to join the search but this brings them in conflict with the locals resulting in physical assaults and even death.

As much as it boosts the local economy, the ecological damage the collection practice puts upon the meadows is immense. In the hurry to collect as many caterpillars as possible, many pick them before the fungus gets a chance to produce spores for reproduction. Some do not hesitate to use unnatural ways of extraction, like setting fires to the surrounding landscape to accelerate the process of melting the snow. The exploitation of the herb beyond sustainable levels has started showing its effect just like it did in Tibet, Nepal and Bhutan where a severe decline in yields was observed. A study of 110 villages of Pithoragarh revealed a 14.81% decline in the Keeda Jadi population in a span of five years[72] which has resulted in a perceptible decline in the harvesting of the herb by the locals. Whereas earlier it was easy to find the herb, today, of all the families who engage in its search, half return empty-handed. Climate change is also to blame, as the snow under which the caterpillar fungus develops is reducing every year. The forest department has tried to regulate the trade by empowering local Van Panchayats to issue licences for collection and become the only entity to whom the herb can be sold under the law. But the enforcement has been weak, as people simply continue with their old ways of collection and sell to middlemen who offer high prices. The overexploitation of this rare fungus has prompted its inclusion in the International Union for Conservation of Nature's (IUCN) red list of threatened species in 2020. In the absence of a sustainable regulation model, the exploitation of Keeda Jadi is sure to result in its extinction in the near future.

The Sacred Offerings

In the Hindu month of *Bhadon* (August–September), the people of Johar Valley in Pithoragarh start preparing for the most awaited festival of *Nanda Ashtami.* Two days prior to the start of the festival, the village community selects two people and entrusts them with the important task of gathering the holy *Brahma Kamal* from the sacred alpine meadows. The next day's schedule for these men is filled with rituals and observances; they must wake before dawn, take a bath in freezing water, dress in all-white clothes and carry fruits with them as an offering to the presiding deity of Bugyal as they walk towards their destination barefoot. Upon reaching the meadow, they first worship the local deity, requesting his permission to collect the treasured flower, after which they begin their search. Only fully mature Brahma Kamals are selected and plucked with extreme care. In older times, even the act of plucking thc flower was believed to be harmful to the plant, so the plucking of each flower was done with teeth with the belief that they can carry out the act only by behaving like an aimal.

The alpine meadows are intimately connected with many traditional religious systems of local communities. The peaks of the Greater Himalaya are dedicated to Lord Shiva. The locals visit the nearest Bugyals, which offer a clear view of the sacred peaks, to worship them. Similarly, many traditional festivals are either organised in the Bugyals, like *Chipla Kedar Jat*, or the Bugyals form an important *padav* (halt) of a larger procession *(jat)*. For example, Bedni Bugyal is the terminating point of the annual Nanda Devi Jat which

Figure 49 The garland of ban tulsi for offering at Badrinath

locals believe to be the site where the Goddess Nanda slayed the demon Mahishasura. In the high-altitude villages where these meadows are located, a tradition of offering different flowers which bloom during the season to the local temples is prevalent. For example, it is a norm to make an offering of Brahma Kamal to the deities of Badrinath and Kedarnath, and during all the festivals held during the months of August-September, when this rare flower blossoms. Similarly, the sacred *Ban Tulsi* (Origanum vulgare) and the beautiful flowers of Primula stewarti are offered at temples of local deities as well as at Badrinath and Kedarnath during the months of their blooming.

The Alpine Pastures

The alpine meadows, carpeted with grassy vegetation, are used as grazing grounds in the summer by local pastoral communities. Pastoralism has been the dominant economic activity of local communities in the upper reaches of the Himalaya and, every summer, the shepherds, locally called *anwals*, proceed with their livestock to nearby Bugyals. The meadows are covered by a thick blanket of snow throughout the winter months. As spring arrives in April, the snow melts and a fresh crop of emerald grass covers the land. Men drive their animals up these pastures at the start of the summers in March and stay there for the entire duration until winter arrives again, at which point they all descend back to their homes. During their stay, temporary shelters called *kharak* for the shepherds and *chhan* for the livestock are built. Grazing on the nutritious grass of Bugyals is the most productive period for these animals. They yield enormous quantities of milk from which various dairy products are made and sent to villages down the valley for sale.

The pastures, thus, are a significant economic resource, making their management essential. They are jointly owned by villages of that valley, and access to them is regulated through traditional customs and institutions. Earlier, the pastures were divided among village households in proportion to the number of livestock each household owned. A tax collector was appointed by the village council who would keep an eye on the number of animals grazing and would collect tax from shepherds from outside the village for access to the pastures. This ensured equitable distribution and prevented overgrazing. Disputes did occur, and usually revolved around

Figure 50 Mules grazing in the meadow

access; local ballads often recounted tales of such disputes and a lot can be gleaned from them about the way these communities lived. But, in recent years, overgrazing has emerged as a major threat to the Bugyals due to the gradual disappearance of erstwhile methods of regulation.

Traditionally, the grazing livestock consisted of sheep and goats owned by local communities. There are over 1.57 lakh sheep/goats and 7.95 thousand buffaloes, cattle and horses graze in alpine pastures of the state.[73] But lately, the composition of the livestock has changed, with an increase in the number of horses, mules, cattle and buffaloes. The manifold increase in horses and mules is especially seen in meadows popular as trekking destinations. Here, the animals are used to transport camping luggage and people. Similarly, the recent practice of granting permits to outside pastoralists like Van Gujjars, who reside in the Shivalik foothills and graze their cattle and buffaloes in the sensitive Bugyals of

Govind Pashu Vihar National Park, is also causing harm to the fragile ecology.

The government has started taking remedial measures to prevent any further damage to these Bugyals. The High Court has put a ban on overnight stays in Bugyals. Although this is a temporary measure, responsible tourism and ecotourism are going to influence the policies in future. The recent restoration of Dayara Bugyal in 2019 by the forest department raises hope for similar restoration of other Bugyals in pitiful conditions. Working with local communities through institutions like the Van Panchayat and the Biodiversity Management Committee (BMC), the problem of overgrazing and commercial exploitation of medicinal flora can be managed. By taking locals into confidence and spreading awareness, equitable distribution of the benefits of local flora's commercial use can be ensured.

Bugyals are not only biodiversity hotspots but also sensitive ecosystems. The cumulative impact of anthropogenic activities endangers the existence of rare endemic species which have been sparsely documented without any systematic study for their therapeutic potential. Every herb is a probable sanjeevani and can enchant others with its beauty, but this is only be possible when these meadows are saved from unsustainable practices and exploitation.

11

FORESTS: A TALE OF THREE TREES

Frederick Wilson was a British soldier who had deserted the army during the First Anglo-Afghan War of 1842. He fled to the state of Tehri-Garhwal and tried to seek refuge in the court of the king, but was refused. He had no choice but to venture deep into the Himalaya and settle in a place called Harshil, near Gangotri in the Valley of Bhagirathi. There, he fell in love with a local girl named Gulabi and they got married. Together, they lived in the village in a palatial home that still stands today. An ambitious man, Wilson was not satisfied with a peaceful Pahadi life. A self-taught botanist and wildlife enthusiast, he started trading in timber and exotic wildlife products. He also introduced cash crops of apple and *rajma* (red beans) to Harshil.

It was said that Wilson acted as a spy for the British for some time during the sepoy mutiny in 1857 and, in return, was pardoned for his desertion. Now a free man, Wilson realised the potential of the forests located in the upper reaches of the Ganga-Yamuna Valley. These regions had been sparsely populated and were situated away from the royal centres of Srinagar and Tehri. As a result, their forests remained untouched, boasting one of the Himalayan region's finest, largest and most densely packed deodar forests.

Wilson soon went into business as a timber contractor and struck a deal with the king of Tehri. Through clever negotiation tactics, Wilson got large tracts of forests on lease for a period of 15 years for a meagre fee of ₹400, and heavy exploitation followed. The rampant felling of deodar and the resultant timber enabled an export of around 65,00,000 wooden sleepers for railways during the period of 1869-85. Wilson had mastered the art of transporting the felled timber by water, which proved to be a cheaper and easier method of transporting heavy loads from remote mountainous areas to the sawmills located in the plains of Haridwar. Obsessed with making profit, he didn't even leave the regional wildlife alone. A trophy hunter, he hunted many exotic animals for their pelts, horns and other products. The unspoiled forests and landscape were soon denuded along with the wildlife inhabiting them.

As a result of this ruthless exploitation, he amassed immense wealth and began living a lavish life. Called Pahari Wilson and the King of Harshil by the locals, he even minted coins in his name which, today, are greatly sought-after by collectors and enthusiasts. Wilson, now a member of the elite wealthy class, shifted from Harshil to Mussoorie to mingle with the English officers and gentry of the British class. There, he became friends with famous authors O. Hume and

Rudyard Kipling, and the latter's story, *The Man Who Would Be King*, is said to have been inspired by Wilson's life. In 1865, the lease expired and the control of forests reverted to the Tehri crown. The then British government of the North-Western Provinces (Uttar Pradesh), aware of the economic importance of these forests, successfully negotiated a 20 lease on behalf of Wilson and the relentless, merciless destruction of the forests continued.

Some distance away from Harshil lies the quaint village of Mukhba, Goddess Ganga's winter seat. Every year in the month of November, the image of Ganga is brought from Gangotri to reside here. Nearby is a temple dedicated to Lord Someshwar. He is thought to be a brother of Ganga and his temple is located in a tranquil sacred forest full of majestic deodars.

Wilson's greed had reached such insatiable proportions that in his quest to maximise his profit, he reached the boundary of this sacred grove. The priest of the temple warned him to spare the sacred forest of the deity, but Wilson did not pay any heed to his words and started destroying the trees and wildlife of Someshwar's grove. It is said that Lord Someshwar, speaking through his oracle, cursed him that the wealth for which he was taking such cruel steps would evaporate, his line would die down and no one would carry forward his name. The curse showed its effect and within a few years. Wilson's business suffered and his two sons, one accused of murder and other a fraud, also died. Heartbroken,

Figure 51 The priest of Someshwar temple cursing Wilson

Wilson died a lonely man in 1883. His last surviving descendant was also killed in an air crash, wiping out his bloodline. The life story of Pahadi Wilson best captures the radical differences in the approach of local people and colonial rulers towards forests and was an important event in the history of the management of forests in Uttarakhand.

For the residents of Uttarakhand, forests perform many roles in addition to being valuable resources for food and fodder. There are several forests whose resources remain intact, given their sacred status. These forests, mostly located around temples, are held in reverence by the local

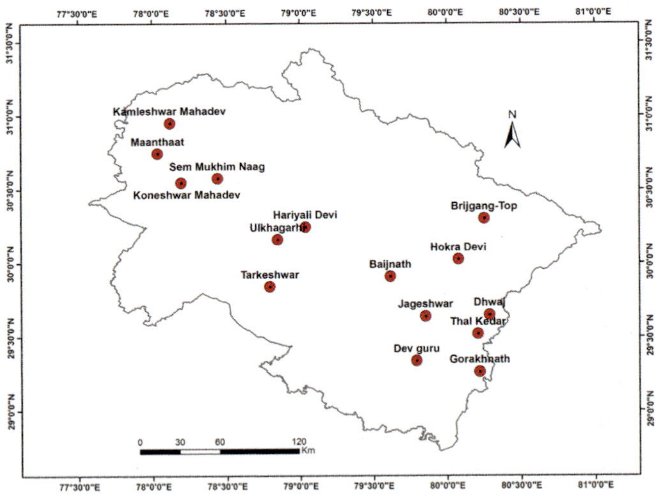

Figure 52 Distribution of prominent sacred groves in the state

people. The institution of sacred groves is based on the belief that the forest and all its resources, including wildlife, belong to the resident deity and, hence, no local or outsider has any right to exploit them. This prevalent belief system ensures that unnatural death and decay in these landscapes is understood as an indicator of misfortune for the community. For example, in the Dudhatoli range, the Divagarhi temple is situated in a healthy oak forest. Locals believe that when anyone harms an oak tree, it oozes blood and a curse is instantly laid upon the offender by an angry deity. Sacred groves are both culturally and environmentally significant, since they are not only connected with the religious beliefs of local communities, but also play an important role in maintaining the local ecosystem and biodiversity. Majority of sacred groves in the state are dominated by either Deodar or Oak trees.

Deodar: God's Own Tree

The deodar, which literally translates to 'God's Wood', has been intimately linked with Lord Shiva since ancient times. Deodar, or cedrus deodara, is a coniferous tree found at altitudes of 2000-3000 metres in the Middle Himalayan ranges. Many Shiva temples in Uttarakhand are located amidst dense deodar forests which are protected by locals from any outside interference. The most well-known deodar sacred groves are the Jageshwar temple complex of Almora and

Figure 53 The sacred grove of Jageshwar temple complex

the Koneshwar Mahadeva grove of Devalsari. A group of 120 small and big temples are clustered in the narrow ravine of Jat Ganga river in a dense forest made purely of Deodar trees. The place is said to be mentioned in the central Shaiva scriptures of the Shiva and Skanda Purana *Daruke vane* or the forest of Deodar. It is believed that some of the most intense manifestations of Shiva occurred in deodar forests. When his consort Sati had burned away her body in the sacrificial fire, Shiva entered the forest, maddened with grief.

In another episode, he came to the forest to teach a lesson to a group of sages who lived in the forest and were engaged in mindless asceticism. They would follow the rituals just for the sake of observing the conventions, without having the spiritual inclination or an emotional bond with Shiva. Thus, when Shiva took the disguise of Kapalika, a naked mendicant with skull as a begging bowl and arrived at their hermitage, the sages did not recognize him. Instead, their chaste wives were attracted towards Kapalika despite his horrible appearance. Least bothered about the interruption of their rituals by the appearance of the mendicant, they were infuriated at his lack of shame and the influence he exerted on their women. In their blind rage, they cursed Kapalika to have his linga fall which plunged the entire universe in darkness. Witnessing the darkness, the sages realised who the mendicant was and how, in their blindness, they could not recognize Shiva. They begged for forgiveness and the linga emerged as a fiery pillar of light with no beginning and no end, restoring the original balance of the universe.

Jageshwar is said to be the place where the above episode happened and a jyotirlinga was established. The Dandeshwar temple is said to mark the place where the *Danda* or curse of the sages took place. Studies by botanists have revealed that in Jageshwar, the earlier landscape of mixed forests was consciously transformed by the Shaiva ascetics into a deodar-dominated grove.[74] Some of these deodar trees are 500-600 years old and the very tall trees with thick girths could even be 1,000 years old.[75] Many of the bifurcated trees are worshipped by the local villagers as a form of *ardhanarishvara*, an incarnation

Figure 54 The co-joined tree of Jageshwar

of Shiva where Shiva and Parvati are shown together as one force.

In the Jaunpur range, 75 kilometres away from Dehradun, is the serene sacred grove of Devalsari famous for its three Bs—birds, butterflies and bees. On the edge of the village Bangshil, in the quiet depths of the pristine deodar forest, lies an ancient temple of Koneshwar Mahadev. Built in a traditional design with a slanting pagoda-like roof, the temple is made of oak, while it stands amidst giant deodars, some of which reach up to heights of 200-250 feet.

The story goes like this—an old ascetic visited the village and wanted a piece of land to build his hut,but the villagers refused. Without saying a word, the ascetic walked uphill and disappeared. Next morning, the villagers were surprised to see young deodars sprouting all over the place in the direction of the disappeared sadhu. He later visited the head priest in a dream and revealed himself as Shiva, who had visited them in disguise. He instructed the priest that between the deodars, at a place where a lone oak grows, he was to build a temple with the branches from that tree.

Figure 55 Koneshwar Mahadev temple surrounded by deodar trees with single oak tree behind

The priest complied, and the temple, dedicated to Shiva, called Koneshwar Mahadeva, stands quiet under the dense canopy of the deodars where it is said to be guarded by a pair of Nagas. A lone oak tree also stands behind the temple, surrounded by deodars on all sides. The deodar tree is endowed with special properties which might have played a role in elevating it to religious status. The wood of the tree is durable and decay-resistant, hence, is frequently used in the construction of temples. It also possesses insect-repellent and anti-fungal properties, due to which local people use it to make boxes for storing food and other valuable items sensitive to insect attacks.

Oak: The Water Wizard

On the way to Badrinath, among the barren peaks, stands an isolated hill covered in dense vegetation. On its summit, is situated a temple dedicated to Hariyali Devi. The given reason for the presence of such rich forestry in an otherwise denuded landscape is that the 5.5 square kilometres of this area fall under the protection of Hariyali Devi, preserved by the locals for centuries. Strict rules govern the entry of people, which include the prohibition of leather items and those who have consumed non-vegetarian foods and alcohol. Any felling of trees and hunting of animals is strictly banned. Only the dead and fallen branches and leaves of trees are permitted

Figure 56 Oak tree

to be used, and those too from the fringes of the forest. The result of such regulation has contributed to the preservation of many indigenous flora and fauna species, making the sanctuary rich in genetic and species diversity. The forest is primarily mixed oak, supporting rare species of oak like *Kharsu* (Quercus semecarpifolia). A survey of floral diversity by a team of researchers recorded the sanctuary harbouring close to 98 different plant species, out of which 82 have medicinal properties while the rest have other economic value (15 timber construction; 19 edible parts). The rich flora supports equally diverse wildlife. Numerous species of bird, butterflies and mammals live in the complex vegetative ecosystem of the grove. Such carefully preserved biodiversity is found in all sacred groves that have been protected against unsustainable development. The locals support the conservation of many endemic species of plants and animals in these groves, which are increasingly becoming threatened in other parts of Uttarakhand. During summers, when many of the water channels run dry, the water needs of the villages located are met by six streams flowing down the Hariyali Devi grove. This ability of the grove to not only preserve biodiversity but also maintain the water profile of the region is partially due to the presence of Oak trees: the water wizards of the Himalaya.

Banj Oak, or quercus leucotrichophora, is the dominant species of oak found at a height of over 2,000 metres in the Himalaya. The mixed temperate forests are characteristic of the Middle Himalayan range and oak trees, interspersed with kafal, rhododendron, and *Angyaar* trees, form the backbone of these forests. Oak supports dense vegetation; one can find a variety of herbs, shrubs and lichens growing beneath its dense canopy, greatly increasing the filtration of rainwater and recharging of aquifers. The roots of the oak are very deep and capable of pulling moisture from great depths to the surface, thus improving soil moisture. Oak forests not only make the weather cooler and wetter, but also guarantee a continuous supply of potable drinking water to nearby villages due to its unique water retention properties. Locals residing in the vicinity of Hariyali Devi are aware of the importance of the oak dominated grove, for they believe that when oak disappears, the streams and rivulets of that region also disappear.

A study was conducted by researchers from the Hemvati Nandan Bahuguna University to compare the quality of surface water in sacred groves with that of nearby regions and assess the impact of the type of forests on water quality.[76] Three sacred groves were selected—Hariyali, Tarkeshwar and Ravigaon. The study found that the water from all the sacred groves met the World Health Organisation (WHO) standards for drinking water, while none of the surrounding areas could pass the test. Among these sites, oak-dominated groves had the best water quality. The study reaffirmed the significant role played by oak forests in maintaining the hydrological profile of the region. Not only are oaks central to the formation and maintenance of Himalayan ecology, but they also form an indispensable part of the livelihood of local communities. Owing to its high-calorific value, its branches burn well and are lopped by villagers to serve as fuel. Its nutrient-rich leaves are gathered by womenfolk to feed their livestock, while the fallen and partially decomposed leaves, rich in nitrogen, are used to fertilise the fields.

Figure 57 Chir-Pine tree

Existing at the same altitude is oak's competitor chir-pine (Pinus Roxburghii). The contrast between oak and pine could not be any greater. Unlike oak, which is a broadleaf tree, pine is a coniferous species whose needle-like leaves are highly flammable. Floral diversity is lowest in pine forests. They contain a single species and do not allow any other trees to grow. Diversity is highest in mixed oak forests, which also support animal and bird biodiversity. Oak thrives in cool and moist weather and, in turn, contributes to maintaining the water profile of the region. Pine needles easily catch fire and are a major contributor to forest fires, although pine can withstand fires and can easily regrow in its aftermath. Today, oak forests are gradually getting replaced by pine. This has far reaching consequences.

What is causing this transformation? This is a long story that encapsulates the broad history of change witnessed by Uttarakhand's forests.

Colonial period: Scientific Forestry

The story starts with the British occupation of India. After the unsuccessful revolt of 1857, the British government sought to leave no stone unturned in preventing any more such uprisings. One key strategy to achieve this goal was to enable faster transportation of military troops to distant places. This led to rapid and extensive laying of railway lines linking British administrative centres with the remotest corners of the country. The demand for wooden sleepers (used in laying railway tracks) increased substantially and, to cater to this demand, a new forest department was set up. Its main task was to identify suitable tree species capable of responding to chemical treatment and possessing rot-resistant properties. Sal and teak forests of the sub montane belt were selected and heavily exploited, leading to severe depletion in their numbers within a few years. The attention then turned to the untouched forests of deodar and pine of the Yamuna and Ganga Valley, the exploitation of which was facilitated by the ruthless contractor Frederick Wilson.

To manage forest resources better, new methods of management were introduced. Scientific forestry found new ground with Dietrich Brandis, a German botanist, who was appointed as the Inspector-General of Forests in India in 1864 and established the Imperial Forest Service the same year, which after independence, became known as Indian Forest Service (IFS). In 1878, he submitted a proposal to the Government to establish a forest school for professional education of forest rangers and foresters, which would open a new chapter in the history of forest management. Government accepted his proposal and an Imperial Forest School was established in Dehradun.

In 1906, the status of the school was raised and it was restructured as Imperial Forest College & Research Institute, with a new staff of six officers from the Imperial Forest Service, each overseeing a specialised branch of forestry. The list included Silviculture, Zoology, Forest Economy, Botany etc. They were assigned the task to conduct research in their respective fields, in addition to teaching the subject to interested students. The college was operating from its

Figure 58 Forest Research Institute, Dehradun

campus at Chandbagh when a decision was made by the forest officers to have a new campus building. Since their service controlled 75% land of British India, they demanded a campus that could rival the newly inaugurated the Viceroy's Palace in New Delhi. Architect C.G Blomfield took the enormous task of designing the magnificent building which was inaugurated by the Viceroy Lord Irwin in 1929.

Today it is known as Forest Research Institute (FRI) and is located in a 1,200-acre campus with huge tree gardens hosting a variety of flora and fauna. A walk in the woods is a must for bird and nature lovers.

This scientific forestry was based on the concept of sustained yield as opposed to indiscriminate felling. Forests were divided into blocks and elaborate working plans were prepared for each block, detailing the annual revenue targets. After all the trees of a block had been felled, the block was closed for regeneration to provide an undisturbed environment for regrowth and to prevent any harm coming to the new saplings. This required controlling the access of locals and their livestock to the forests. Several acts and rules were passed by the British government to control the unchecked activities of villagers and impose restrictions on them. Most notable of them were the Forest Acts of 1865, 1878 and 1927. These acts promulgated by the British government converted open-access areas into protected forests which empowered the British government to declare any area as government forest and make rules to manage the space. As per the Forest Act, 1878, forests were divided into reserved forests (fully under the control of the government), protected forests (partly under the control of the government) and village forests (controlled by villages). The acts were promulgated to ensure that the control of forests remained largely in the hands of the government to maximise economic profits through scientific management of these forests.[77]

The impact of these policies on local communities was immense. The forests with which they once shared intimate relationships and could roam freely in were suddenly out of bounds. Whatever concessions the British granted in the so-called 'protected' and 'village' forests were also based on the assumption that access to these forests was a 'privilege' and not a 'right' of local communities, and could be taken back any time. Rather than giving the whole community access, the British preferred dealing at the individual level. Thus, the forest rules strictly specified the amount of timber and other forest produce an individual household could utilise. This preference for individuals led to the fragmentation of village communities and changed their relationship with the forests. With forests out of their control, the locals increasingly adopted an indifferent attitude, believing that any effort put in to preserve the forests would result in its takeover. If the quality of village forests improved and the forest official came to notice it, he would seize control of that forest as well. People staged protests in various parts of the state against the Tehri King as well as the Kumaon Commissioner to roll back the oppressive laws. These protests culminated into the great uprising of 1921 when locals entered the prohibited forests and set fires to many regenerating blocks. The British suppressed the revolt with some difficulty, but not before suffering a heavy revenue loss. These protests forced the British to rethink its forest policy. They decided to skillfully tweak the policy in such a way that some of the demands of the locals could be accommodated while retaining the same control over the forests as before.

The chief grievances of people related to restricted access to the forests, which led to difficulties in sustaining their livelihood that depended on collecting fuelwood, grazing their livestock and setting fires to bring forth fresh pasture for them.[78] To accommodate these practices, the British approach changed from extensive to intensive one. As Although the oak's ecological and cultural significance was high, its economic potential was low. The wood of oak is not suitable for construction activities and the tree does not produce any commercial products. Hence, for the British, the oak was an inferior species of no use. In contrast, the chir-pine had limited value for the Himalayan ecosystem and local people, but its commercial potential was enormous. Its timber was durable and suitable for railway sleepers. Its bark could be tapped for extracting resin, a by-product which finds extensive use in the turpentine industry. The regenerating blocks were still outside the reach of local people, but they were now directed at mixed forests comprising invaluable species like oak. If locals needed firewood, they were encouraged to lop the branches of oak. They could graze their cattle and goats on the dense vegetation found in these forests, indirectly clearing the litter and paving way for the colonisation by the pine species. Forest fires were another special headache for forest officials. The solution, they arrived upon, involved the forest department itself conducting controlled burnings at designated places, while locals were allowed to use fire during non-fire season and under careful watch of officials. The set of strategies adopted by the British encouraged villagers to use oak-dominated mixed forests for their livelihood and, in the process, facilitated the growth of commercially valuable chir-pine trees and turned mixed forests into pure standing forests. Overall, a win-win situation for the British.

VAN PANCHAYAT

One of the by-products of the 1921 protests was the creation of the institution of Van Panchayat (forest council) in the same year, which was given the responsibility of framing the rules for the day-to-day management of forests under the control of villages.

Post-Independence: Chipko Movement

The forest laws promulgated by the British and the extensive bureaucracy established to enforce those laws were retained by the Indian government after Independence and continued to be a major source of conflict between state and people. The discontent of the people burst forth in the early 1970s, when the impact of huge scale deforestation on local ecology became apparent. The heavy monsoon rains triggered massive destructive flash floods and landslides which caused immense ruin and washed away people, crops and livestock. The damage was particularly severe in the Alaknanda Valley and the tributaries of the river overflowed their banks. It did not take long for people to realise the link between large scale felling of trees and the magnitude of the disaster. The worst-hit villages were the ones which were located below the forests where the contractors had started their tree-cutting operations. The grievances of the people were channelled through the Dasholi Gram Swarajya Sangh (DGSS), an organisation formed by local activist Chandi Prasad Bhatt on the issue of local employment, and active in Chamoli since the 1960s.

The tipping point came in 1973, when the forest department awarded the right to cut ash wood to a sports manufacturing company, Symonds and Co., and rejected the Sangh's demand of ten ash trees which they needed to make their farm tools. This injustice led to mass demonstrations and protests by local people. When deciding on the methods of protest—options for which included burning the forest timber depots and lying on the road in front of trucks—Chandi Prasad Bhatt suggested that they should hug the trees instead. Hence, the Chipko movement was born. The villagers of Mandal took an oath to not leave the trees even if the axes of contractors split open their stomachs. They succeeded in turning the company away without letting them cut a single tree. Symonds was allotted an alternate forest block of Phata, this time in the Mandakini Valley. When the news reached the DGSS, they contacted the Phata village and organised a successful protest which led to Symonds leaving empty-handed again.

But the government was not going to give up easily. It held its yearly auction of new forest plots in November 1973, and the forest block of Reni village near Joshimath was the first to be allotted to a contractor. When the felling was due, in March 1974, the men of Reni and nearby villages were called to Gopeshwar, the capital of Chamoli district, to collect the compensation for their land taken by the army after the 1962 war. While the men were away, the contractor arrived in Reni, assured of not facing any more trouble. But he was wrong. The women of the village, led by Gaura Devi, saw the labourers ready with their implements, rushed to the scene and stuck themselves to the trees, not letting go despite many abuses and threats. At some places, like Pindar Valley, while the local men were lured by the prospects of commercialisation and agreed to supply labour for felling of oak trees, it was the women who resisted the decision and protested.

Women were the worst affected as they had to bear the burden of collecting fuel and fodder for household needs. And for the women of Pindar Valley, the forest, marked for felling, was the only source of wood and fodder near their village. If all the trees of this forest were cut, the women would be forced to walk several miles in their search. Their concerns went unheeded, and it was only with the intervention of the Chipko activists that the decision of felling was reversed. So angry was the village headman that he threatened the activists to never show their face there again. The disruptions caused at the auctions and felling operations finally forced the then chief minister of Uttar Pradesh, H.N. Bahuguna, to take cognizance of the issue.

He formed a committee to investigate the matter. The team included scientists, members of the DGSS and secretaries of state. The committee found that the major reason behind the devastation of the 1970 floods was widespread deforestation of river Alaknanda's catchment area. The committee findings resulted in the ban on commercial felling of trees for ten years in the upper basin of the Alaknanda Valley.

The people of Alaknanda basin (Chamoli) had won a hard fight. Seeing their success, the Chipko movement spread to other parts of Garhwal and Kumaon. In Tehri, the flooding of Bhagirathi Valley in 1978 had caused much devastation. Despite this, auctions were held as usual, angering people. Uniting under the leadership of activist Sunderlal Bahuguna, who went on a hunger strike, the movement quickly spread, with men, women and children keeping night vigils to thwart any attempts by contractors to cut down trees. Bahuguna blamed Pahadi Wilson and the British for causing such great damage to the forests of Garhwal. He was jailed, but not before becoming an inspiration for non-violent protests at several places. The Chipko *Andolan* (movement) was a mixed success. It heightened the consciousness of people regarding the importance of forests and their rights to it and forced the forest department and the government to recognise these rights, even if on paper, through decentralised and participatory approach under the Joint Forest Management. The intensive rules framed under the new laws were rarely followed in practice and, at some places, hindered developmental activities, such as the requirement of an elaborate permission process for building schools, hospitals or any other infrastructure on forest land.

The commercialisation and felling of trees continued until people, especially women, rose in protest. The Chipko movement in the 1970s once again brought to fore the debate of commercialisation vs conservation. The balance tilted in favour of conservation, and it was widely acknowledged that proper conservation of forests is possible only by according greater role and voice to local communities. Hence, in the 1990s, the concept of Joint Forest Management was introduced and Van Panchayats set out to empower local communities in the management of forest resources. Despite such measures, the forest quality of Uttarakhand is showing worrying signs.

The processes and policies set in motion by the British decades ago snowballed and their impact continues to be felt even today. Change in the composition of species of a landscape over a long period is called ecological succession. Oak is a keystone species, while pine is a pioneer species. In the Himalayan ecosystem, natural succession moves from pine forests to pine-oak forests and eventually oak forests. However, this natural succession is disturbed by human intervention through activities like fire, lopping, grazing, etc. In the Himalaya, British policies had changed these dynamics and oak forests, which is the late successional species, got replaced by pine forests, thus, turning the clock back on natural succession.

A joint study on the patterns of the expansion of chir-pine trees and their gradual replacement of traditional oak forests was conducted by the Centre for Ecology Development and Research (CEDAR), IISc, Bengaluru and the National Remote Sensing Centre.[79] The study found that oak forests in Uttarakhand have reduced by 29%, while pine forests increased by up to 74% in the span of 26 years, from 1991 and 2017.

The causes behind this phenomenon are many, but the chief reason is the difference in the germination and growth of oak and pine saplings. Oak seeds need a shady and moist environment for germination. These seeds are sensitive to heat and become unviable under direct sunlight and dry conditions. Even if the acorn germinates, it will take a long time to mature and achieve adult height, with some taking ten years to achieve a height of six inches. This slow growth rate, coupled with increasing forest fires, is slowly hindering the renewal of existing oak forests and emergence of new ones. Due to climate change, hot and dry summers have become the norm, making it very easy for the flammable chir-pine litter to catch fire. This fire, if not controlled quickly, can spread throughout the mountain side fanned by the wind. As oak forests exist in the same belt as chir-pine, they are worst hit by the fires, which suck up all the soil moisture. Oaks are the keystone species on whom other species depend for survival. Disappearance of oak forests does not bode well for the biodiversity of birds, animals and flora which, together, have maintained a healthy ecosystem. With the disappearance of oak, the fragile ecology of the Himalaya will be negatively affected.

To check the degradation of jungles and depleting water resources, local villagers have taken it upon themselves to protect them. A new trend of dedicating village forests to the local deity is becoming common in the Kumaon districts of Bageshwar and Pithoragarh. Ten years ago, the village of Malla Ghorpatta in Munsyari Pithoragarh was known for its rich greenery, but when the development activities and unregulated felling started affecting the forests, the villagers jointly decided to dedicate them to the local deity, Purbyal. This resulted in restrictions on lopping and grazing of animals on forest land. Within five years, the forests returned to their original condition. Similarly, in Bageshwar, two villages decided to dedicate the vanishing jungles near

Figure 59 The highly flammable needles of Chir-Pine tree

them to Kotgiri Devi. The decision was written down on legal stamp paper and signed by the villagers before being taken to the temple, where it was displayed for the public, all in an effort to inform the visitors of the ownership of the forests and caution them against harming the greenery. Flags and poles were also erected to mark the precise boundaries of the forests.

The jungles of Uttarakhand have played an important role in the lives of people who reside in their vicinity. This symbiotic relation between the forests and locals came under extreme stress with the disastrous policies of the colonial empire, and continued by the government post-independence. Although attempts were made by the government to address the growing challenge of degrading forests and the rights of locals over forests, it is now being gradually realised that long term sustainable conservation is not possible without community participation.

12

WILDLIFE: THE MAN-EATER AND THE HUNTER

In the summer of 1938, a man-eating tiger became active and started terrorizing the people of the Ladhya Valley situated on the borders of Kumaon and Nepal. In the village of Kot Kindri, it carried off a girl who was busy collecting mangoes that had fallen from a tree. After a few days, the man-eater struck again and this time, its victim was an unfortunate woman. She was cutting the brushwood between her terraced fields while her son was working in the fields below. The tiger sprang from above and took her away. So sudden was the attack that the woman got only a single chance to scream. Her son, who witnessed the attack, informed the village headmen. He gathered around 80 men, and the party left to search the jungle, finding only torn clothes and a few bones. These recurrent attacks got the administration worried, as the forest department had marked the trees of that region for felling in November. If the man-eater was not restrained, the contractors would not be able to secure labour and the contracts would have to be cancelled. Keeping both its revenue and the safety of the people in mind, the then deputy Commissioner of Kumaon, Sir William Ibbotson, called the famous tiger hunter Jim Corbett to hunt this beast.

JIM CORBETT

Edward James Corbett, better known as Jim Corbett, was a hunter and conservationist who became an authority on wildlife, especially tigers. Born to British parents in Nainital in 1875, he worked as a fuel inspector and contractor with the Bengal and North-Western Railways in the 1890s and early 1900s. In 1907, his successful shooting of the Champawat man-eater, who had killed 400 people, brought him fame as a hunter who was called upon by the district administration whenever a man-eater started terrorizing the locals.

Arriving in the village of Thak where the tigress had secured its latest victim, Corbett studied the pugmarks it had left behind, trying to gain information about its age, sex and walking patterns. He first tried to catch the tigress using what was known as the standard hunting method. Fat buffaloes or goats were used as bait to attract predators while the hunter hid in a secure location, waiting for the tiger to take the bait. However, this method proved unsuccessful as the tigress did not even touch the buffaloes. Meanwhile, a man from the village went missing. He had gone out of his house to check on his cattle and had not returned since. A small team led by Corbett, Ibbotson, and a few men from the village took off on the trail and, through his careful observation of pugmarks and various other markers, Corbett was successful in tracking down the partially eaten body of the man. He even found the rock behind which the tigress lay, but she fled as soon as she sensed people approaching. Believing that the tigress would return to the body, Corbett decided to spend the night in a nearby tree and wait for her. Ibbotson and his men brought the material to build a *machan* (a makeshift platform on the tree), upon which Corbett secured himself to hunt the tigress while the rest of the team started for the village.

The sun had set and darkness was soon to follow. Corbett lit his cigarette and listened carefully. He knew that the tigress was close by. Ten minutes had passed since Ibbotson and his party had left when a monkey, who had been silent all this time, started calling. Similarly, a *kakar* deer also started barking hysterically at a distance. Judging by these sounds, Corbett deduced correctly that instead of coming back for the dead body, the tigress had gone after Ibbotson and his party. He spent all night listening to the movement of the tigress in the valley down below, praying anxiously for his friend's safety. Fortunately, Ibbotson had also realised the danger and kept the group closer. As a result, while the tigress had followed them all the way down to the village, she was unable to catch any of them.

In the next few days, Corbett tried various methods to catch her, techniques that had been successful in his previous hunts, but all in vain. The tigress was intelligent and careful. Throughout all his time spent hunting, Corbett could not even catch a glimpse of the animal, let alone shoot her. He spent many sleepless nights waiting for her to show up, resulting in his health getting affected. When his sister, Maggie, began worrying about his health and called him home, Corbett went back to Nainital. The tigress resumed killing and the entire village of Thak had to flee, leaving the place deserted.

Three weeks later, Corbett returned. This time, he vowed to kill the man-eater in the next ten days or quit hunting for good. Soon, nine days had passed and Corbett was nowhere near catching the tigress. Instead, he had to be on constant alert since the fresh pugmarks indicated that the tigress was, in fact, on his trail.

On the tenth day, after another unsuccessful night of trying to lure the tigress with bait, Corbett was returning to the village accompanied by his men and the goats, when he heard the roar of the tigress coming from somewhere deep in the jungle. From his experience, he understood that it was a mating call and made a spur-of-the-moment decision to lure the tigress out. He mimicked the mating call of a male tiger! The effect was instantaneous, and the tigress answered his call with one of her own. Her roars grew closer and Corbett frantically searched for a suitable location from which to

Figure 60 Corbett shooting the man-eater tigress

shoot her. Dusk had fallen. The light was rapidly fading, it would be nightfall in a few minutes, and Corbett and his entourage would be left at the mercy of their ferocious nemesis. Corbett found a big rock and perched delicately on it, with his finger on the trigger. The men accompanying him crouched behind the rock, frozen with fear at the sounds of the man-eater inching closer and closer. Thick foliage hindered Corbett's vision, and he could only make an intelligent guess as to the direction from which the tigress would emerge. With no more than thirty seconds of daylight left, Corbett called once again. The tigress came running out of the bushes into the open and stopped in surprise, seeing the hunter instead of a tiger. Corbett seized his chance and shot her in the head. The recoil from the gun was so strong that it hit his jaw, sending him spiralling backwards on the top of his men. He recovered quickly and fired two more shots at the tiger. Finally, the man-eater was dead. The news of the man-eater's death spread like wildfire when the locals carried her body to the nearest village. People returned to their homes and Thak was populated once again.

Tigers are one of the most charismatic animals of the wild, inspiring awe and terror at the same time. Apex predators of their territories, tigers can be found in diverse ecosystems, from the cold and windy Siberia to the tropical marshlands of the Sundarbans and Java. In the Indian subcontinent, the subspecies known as the Bengal Tiger is found to inhabit diverse landscapes, but its most prominent location is in the Shivalik-Terai foothills of the Himalaya, stretching all the way from the Yamuna in the west to Brahmaputra in the northeast. Tigers of the Terai belt are larger than average, weighing more than 400 pounds and some recording the length of 10 feet or 3.23 metres (the man-eater of Powalgarh was the largest seen by Corbett). The tiger's strength is legendary. Its teeth and claws can crush the bones of its prey with ease.

A few years ago, a video went viral on the internet. A female tiger had strayed outside the boundaries of the Kaziranga National Park. Park rangers were deployed to tranquillise it and bring the her back. Mounted atop an elephant, they were searching for it in the high grasses when the roaring tigress, hiding in the grass, leaped so high that, with one single stroke, she managed to shred open the arm of *mahout* (a person who rides and tends the elephant), making him lose three fingers in the process.

The tiger's teeth are dangerous tools as well. Nature has evolved them in such a way that tigers can crush the thick, muscle-bound necks of its prey and are able to carry the heavy, lifeless mass across long distances with ease. Preferring wild buffaloes and deer-sambar as their choice of prey, tigers avoid dealing with humans unless they pose a threat to their or their cubs' well-being. Seen in this context, the frequency of man-eaters operating during Corbett's period in the early twentieth century comes as a surprise.

What caused so many tigers to shed their natural aversion towards humans and adopt a new predatory behaviour erstwhile alien to them?

The answer lay in the number of processes set in motion by British colonists to maximise their profit from the land they had conquered. The successful transformation of the malaria-ridden and waterless tract of Terai and Bhabar into irrigated and populated landmass by Sir Henry Ramsay in the late nineteenth century set the stage for future man-wild conflicts. After successfully introducing irrigation in the area, the felling of trees was started by contractors to make space for new settlement. The story of the man-eater of Kumaon occurred, against this backdrop. The growing demand for wood for railway sleepers was met initially by the sub montane forests of sal and haldu trees found aplenty in the Kumaon foothills. So relentless was the lopping that, by the turn of the new century, these forests were severely depleted and the demand was now being met by felling pristine forests of deodar and pine growing on higher altitudes.

Hunting used to be a means of entertainment for royalty of yore, but increasingly became a past-time for common British officers and their group of friends. With introduction and easy access to hunting rifles, these were increasingly adopted by the villagers as means of protection while venturing into the jungle. In Corbett's experience, in nine out of ten cases, a tiger was forced to become a man-eater when it could no longer catch its natural prey owing to wounds received from gunshots or while killing a porcupine. In one case, the tigress became severely wounded when around fifty quills got embedded in her leg as she tried to eat a porcupine. When trying to extract the quills, she lost her teeth while the quills broke and got embedded more deeply in her skin. As she lay wounded in the tall grass, a woman from a nearby village started cutting the grass. Annoyed, the tigress killed her, earning herself the moniker of man-eater. The easy availability of dead human bodies was another factor that gave the tigers a taste of human flesh, and when they didn't have access to dead bodies anymore for one reason or the other, they took to active hunting. The tigers of Sunderbans lost their aversion to humans long ago by eating the human bodies regularly thrown into the jungle by the recurring cyclones.

It is not just tigers who are prone to becoming man-eaters. There are cases of other carnivores, like leopards becoming dreaded man hunters as well. In the deadly case of the 'man-eater of Rudraprayag', a leopard killed close to 400 people on the pilgrimage route, (located on the way between Kedarnath and Badrinath) and remained elusive for a long time. It was an expert in evasion, and it was with great difficulty and luck that Corbett neutralised it.

However, the hunting strategy adopted by man-eater leopards differs from man-eater tigers in some aspects, like the timing of their attack.

While a tiger hunts during daytime, a leopard prefers at the night. A man-eating tiger loses all its fear of humans but a leopard, even a man-eater, is still fearful of humans. It moves stealthily through the village while on the hunt and is smart enough to silently break open the door of a house and grab its unsuspecting prey, immobilising him in an instant. Those sleeping next to the victim or in the same room do not even realise that someone has disappeared. Leopards are scavengers by nature. Hence, most often, they become man-eaters after eating a dead human body.

Generally, a dead body is cremated on the banks of a river. But in unusual circumstance, during an epidemic for instance, when the number of dead bodies increases, arranging fuelwood and labour to carry bodies for kilometres to the river can become a cumbersome task. In such cases, another method of disposal is used where a live burning coal is put inside the mouth of the dead and the body thrown over the cliff into the valley where it becomes food for the leopards. Once the pandemic is over, the supply of dead bodies is cut off, forcing the predator to take to deliberately killing humans.

Corbett witnessed this in two such cases. In the Rudraprayag man-eater case, the leopard became active just after the cholera epidemic had ravaged the countryside in the early 1900s and the man-eater leopard of Pannar followed soon after the influenza epidemic of 1918.

The public paranoia caused by these man-eaters was extreme. People suspected that the man-eater was not an animal but a shape-shifting man who would plot his schemes carefully and execute them. In one case in Rudraprayag, a sadhu was nearly lynched by an angry mob when they accused him of turning into a leopard and killing people to satisfy his lust for human flesh. The district Commissioner of Gadwal,

Philip Mason, saved the sadhu and convinced the crowd to put him under house arrest and keep a close watch on him. When an attack happened while the sadhu was imprisoned, the crowd believed his innocence and let him go. Near the Nainital hills, the kills were frequently attributed to the Boksas who lived in the forests of Bhabar-Terai. The motive ascribed to them was the theft of the victims' valuable items and jewellery. This reasoning perpetuated because more women than men had been killed by these man-eaters.

THE DENIZENS OF KUMAON FORESTS

Although it is his hunts that have earned Corbett fame, he is also known for vividly describing other denizens of the forests in his memoirs. The Indian Muntjac, also called *kakar* locally, is the smallest of all deer species, including the sambar and the spotted deer found in the forests. Despite being small, their distinct harsh call can be heard a kilometre away and is often used to raise alarm whenever the deer spots a carnivore. On numerous occasions, Corbett had relied on a kakar's call to gauge the direction and movement of the tiger through the forests. The Himalayan bear is another regular member of the Kumaon forests. Possessing a sensitive nose, it would often enter the village in search of honey. Bears feared no one, and Corbett witnessed a rare fight between a tiger and a bear, when the bear tried to snatch the tiger's kill from it. The fat of dead bears is a highly valued commodity in Kumaon households, where people use it as a cure of rheumatism.

But what made Corbett different from other hunters? And why is he referred to as a hunter-conservationist—an oxymoron? In his thirty-two-year-long career, Corbett shot 33 man-eaters, 31 tigers and two leopards, all in the state of Uttarakhand. Addressed as Carpet Sahib by the locals, his hunting of man-eaters by putting his own life at risk led to the locals viewing him reverentially as a sadhu. He penned his experiences in his book, *Man-Eaters of Kumaon*, which continues to be hugely popular. After India gained independence in 1947, Corbett left the country with his sister Maggie and went to Kenya, where he published his second book, *The Man-Eating Leopard of Rudraprayag* and began writing his third, titled *My India*, a collection of short stories about the land he fondly remembered and its people with whom he had interacted and forged closed friendships. But it was in his book *Jungle Lore*, the least known of his books, that we finally get a peek into how Corbett developed a wide knowledge of and established a close relationship with the natural world which helped him successfully hunt such dangerous beasts.

As a child, Corbett used to spend hours observing and studying nature around his home in Kaladhungi located in the foothills. At first, distinguishing the footprints of different animals was difficult, but by carefully observing the foot impressions made by animals crossing the river in the wet sand, he was able to spot minor differences and devised thumb rules to identify the species from its tracks. For instance, he learned that the animals like dogs, that chase their prey, have bigger toes in relation to their paws, while those which stalk their prey—like cats, tigers, etc—have smaller toes relative to their paws. During hunts, Corbett could tell the species, age and sex of the man-eater by simply studying their tracks and could stalk the animal for miles by following its tracks. By hearing the calls made by different birds and animals during childhood, he soon learnt to imitate them. So accurate was his mimicking that animals, when hearing him call, would follow him. This advantage allowed Corbett to lure the man-eater out in the open by giving out a mating call, a strategy which allowed Corbett to outsmart the clever Thak tigress. Corbett also cultivated his sense of hearing, which allowed him to follow the invisible movement of tigers and leopards in dense vegetation or during night.

The hunting of the Thak man-eater on November 30, 1938, was the last hunt of Jim Corbett, which he accomplished at the age of 63. No longer in his prime, his growing concerns for the dwindling population of tigers made Corbett replace his gun with a camera. In his home at Kaladhungi, he set up a jungle studio and started the first cine-photography of tigers, where he went on to shoot many exotic and beautiful pictures of animals in the wild. Corbett was the first to realise the significance of the tiger in the maintenance of the forest's ecosystem and the need to check the indiscriminate hunting of this animal.

During the early 1930s, he published articles in the government publication *Review of the Week* which spelt out Corbett's conservationist stance and served to make the public aware of the decreasing population of tigers near villages. He encouraged sportsmen to replace their guns with cameras, expounding the benefits of the latter over the former.

In 1907, Sir Michael Keen proposed that the forest of Kumaon be the host to a wildlife sanctuary, but the idea did not find much ground at the time. But in 1934, the governor of the United Provinces, Sir Malcolm Hailey, under whose territory this region lay, carried this idea forward. He rooted for the idea of a wildlife sanctuary here and called for stringent laws to ensure the protection of local flora and fauna. He entrusted the task of determining the sanctuary boundaries to Corbett, who was the best and the most knowledgeable person for the job. Finally, in 1936, the United Province National Park Act was enacted and this reserved forest became the first national park of India, named Hailey National Park. Later, in 1955, it was renamed Ramganga National Park, but upon Corbett's death, the government changed the name the same year to honour his legacy. The Corbett National Park became known for its tigers, a species around which global awareness has only increased. In 1973, the government of India launched Project Tiger to check the declining tiger population and raise awareness about the conservation of this majestic animal. The park became the first Tiger Reserve of India in 1973 and today out of 53 tiger reserves of India, it has the highest tiger population.

TABLE OF FIGURES

SELECTED BIBLIOGRAPHY

1. Agarwal, Deepa. *Journey to the Forbidden City*. India Puffin, 2020, p. 152.
2. Atkinson, Edwin Thomas. *The Himalayan Gazetteer, Or, The Himalayan Districts of the North Western Province of India*. natraj publishers, 2014, p. 2631.
3. Budhwar, Kusum. *Where Gods Dwell*. Penguin Books India, 2010, p. 296.
4. Chanchani, Nachiket. *Mountain Temples and Temple Mountains*. University of Washington Press, 2019, p. 288.
5. Corbett, Jim. *Man-Eaters of Kumaon*. Rupa Publications India, 2016, p. 236.
6. Corbett, Jim. *The Jim Corbett Omnibus*. OUP India, 1991.
7. Debroy, Bibek. *The Mahabharata*. Penguin Books India, 2012, p. 648.
8. Debroy, Bibek. *The Mahabharata: Sections 16 to 32*. Penguin Classics, 2010, p. 528.
9. Ghosha, Cañcalakumāra. *Ganga*. Niyogi Books Pvt. Ltd, 2019, p. 284

10. Guha, Ramachandra. *The Unquiet Woods.* 1989, p. 250.
11. Huckelbridge, Dane. *No Beast So Fierce.* HarperCollins, 2019, p. 304.
12. Kak, Manju. *In the Shadow of the Devi Kumaon.* Niyogi Books, 2018, p. 256.
13. Keay, John. *The Great Arc.* HarperCollins, 2010, p. 244.
14. Mittal, Arun K. *British Administration in Kumaon Himalayas.* Mittal Publications, 1986, p. 249.
15. Negi, Chandra S. *In the Garb of Nanda Devi Raj Jaat.* Winsar Publishing Company Dehradun, 2013.
16. Negi, S. S. *Discovering the Himalaya.* Indus Publishing, 1998.
17. Niśańka, Rameśa Pokhariyāla. *Himalayan Mahakumbh.* Pilgrims Publishing, 2012, p. 256.
18. Ohri, Lokesh. *Till Kingdom Come.* State University of New York Press, 2021, p. 416.
19. Pande, Vikrant, and Neelesh Kulkarni. *In The Footsteps Of Rama.* Harper Collins, 2021, p. 272.
20. Sax, William Sturman. *Dancing the Self.* Oxford University Press on Demand, 2002, p. 236.
21. Sax, William Sturman. *Mountain Goddess.* Oxford University Press on Demand, 1993, p. 246.
22. Varma, Pavan K. *Adi Shankaracharya.* Westland Publication Limited, 2018, p. 354.
23. Wallis, Christopher D. *Tantra Illuminated.* 2022, p. 516.
24. Whitmore, Luke. *Mountain, Water, Rock, God.* University of California Press, 2018.

IMAGE CREDITS

1.	Uttarakhand Tourism Development Board	18, 21, 53
2.	Lokesh Ohri, Been There Doon That	22, 32 (a)
3.	Gajendra Singh	4, 9, 15, 24, 31, 32 (b & c), 43, 44, 46, 47, 48, 49, 50, 52, 56
4.	Neha Mittal	34, 40, 55, 57, 58, 59
5.	Amit Gautam	38
6.	Amod Uniyal	45
7.	Sachin Uniyal	54
8.	Prabir Dey	35, 25
9.	Pooja Saklani	3, 6, 8, 13, 14, 17, 27, 41
10.	Bhumesh Bharti	23

All illustrative figures by Pooja Saklani

NOTES

1 http://www.uttaranchaltourism.in/yoga-in-Himalaya.html

2 Rāya, Pratāpacandra, and Kisari Mohan Ganguli. *The Mahabharata of Krishna-Dwaipayana Vyasa Translated Into English Prose: Anuçasana parva (1893)*. Vol. 9. Bhārata Press, 1893.

3 Different terms referring to sages, ascetics and accomplished hermits.

4 Mishra, Ishita. "Char-Dham yatra sees record footfall this year". The Hindu. October 13, 2022. https://www.thehindu.com/news/national/other-states/char-dham-yatra-sees-record-footfall-this-year/article66001254.ece

5 Rāya et al.. *The Mahabharata, Section 111, Udyoga Parva*

6 Rāya et al. *The Mahabharata.* Section 111, Udyoga Parva

7 Rāya et al. *The Mahabharata.* Book 1: Adi Parva: Section I

8 Rāya et al.

9 Jain, Anita. "बद्रीनाथ धाम जहां माता लक्ष्मी ने लिया बदरी वृक्ष का रुप, जानिए बद्रीनाथ धाम से जुडी रोचक पौराणिक बातें [Badrinath dham where Goddess Laxmi took form as a Badri tree, discover Puranic tales about Badrinath]". Amar Ujala. June 15,

2023. https://www.amarujala.com/spirituality/religion/badrinath-temple-history-in-hindi-facts-about-uttrakhand-badrinath-temple-2023-06-15

10 Debroy, Bibek. *The Mahabharata: Volume 2* Vol. 2. Penguin UK, 2015.

11 Ganguli, Kisari M. *The Mahabharata.* Otbebookpublishing, 2021. Book 3: Vana Parva: Tirtha-yatra Parva: Section XC

12 Eck, Diana L. *India: A Sacred Geography.* Harmony, 2012.

13 Tagore G. V. *"Bhagavata Purana."* New Delhi: Motilal Banarsidass. 1950.

14 Ganguli, Kisari M. *The Mahabharata.*

15 As narrated by Rajan Prasad Dimri, the priest at Pandukeshwar.

16 Ghatak, Ashis. "*Path to God: Trekking up Uttarakhand to Satopanth.*" Outlook Traveller. March 13, 2019. https://www.outlookindia.com/outlooktraveller/explore/story/69422/path-to-god-trekking-up-uttarakhand-to-satopanth

17 Ganguli, Kisari M. *The Mahabharata.*

18 Shastri J. L. *"The Shiva Purana."* New Delhi: Motilal Banarsidass. 1950.

19 Whitmore, Luke. *Mountain, Water, Rock, God.* University of California Press, 2018.

20 *Adi Shankaracharya: Hinduism's Greatest Thinker* by Pavan K Varma is a good book to start for anyone wishing to learn more about the life of Adi Shankaracharya.

21 The story can be found in *A Sacred Journey: The Kedar Kalpa: Series of Pahari paintings and the painter Purkhu of Kangra* by Karuna Goswamy and B.N Goswamy.

22 Ganguli, Kisari M. *The Mahabharata.*

23 Suryavanshi (solar) and Chandravanshi (lunar) are two principal lineages of Hindu mythology.

24 Raper, Felix Vincent. "*Narrative of a Survey for the Purpose of Discovering the Sources of the Ganges.*" Asiatic Researches 11 (1812): 446-564.

25 Herald, A. Donald. "*Gungotree: The Holy Shrine of Mahadeo*". https://www.donaldheald.com/pages/books/31292/james-baillie-fraser/gungotree-the-holy-shrine-of-mahadeo

26 Ganguli, Kisari M. *The Mahabharata.*

27 Debroy, Bibek. *The Mahabharata.*

28 Ganguli, Kisari M. *The Mahabharata.*

29 Ganguli, Kisari M. *The Mahabharata.*

30 Ganguli, Kisari M. *The Mahabharata.*

31 Dubey, D. P. *"Kumbh Mela: Do our Vedic texts mention this unique pilgrimage."* Sahapedia. January 28, 2019. https://www.sahapedia.org/kumbh-mela-do-our-vedic-texts-mention-unique-pilgrimage#:~:text=Indeed%2C%20this%20festival%20does%20not,churned%20the%20ocean%20(samudramanthan).

32 Pokharial, Ramesh. *Maha Kumbh Biggest Planet Event (A Managerial Perspective*). (Diamond Pocket Books Pvt Ltd, 2022).

33 *Negi, R.S. "Rupkund Human Remains: A Mystery Yet Unresolved.*" IGNCA.

34 Budhwar, Kusum. "*Where Gods Dwell.*" Penguin Books India, 2010, p. 296.

35 Pant, Rajshekhar. "*Skeleton Lake: What happens when ice melts in the Roopkund tarn?*" Down To Earth. August 31, 2005. https://www.downtoearth.org.in/coverage/skeleton--lake-100325.

36 Pappas, Stephanie. "*Hundreds of Skeletons Fill this Remote Himalayan Lake. How Did They Get There?*" Live Science. February 24, 2021. https://www.livescience.com/roopkund-skeleton-lake-mystery.html.

37 Keay, John. *The Great Arc: The Dramatic Tale of How India was Mapped and Everest was Named* (HarperCollins, 2000).

38 "*Story of the Nanda Devi sanctuary: The abode of the Goddess*" by Harish Kapadia.com.

39 Shipton, Eric; Tilman, W. H, "*Nanda Devi: Exploration and Ascent*" (Mountaineers Books, 2000).

40 Shipton, et al. *Nanda Devi.*

41 Another word for mait.

42 Sax, S. William, "*Chaya Maya: The Songs and Journeys of Nanda Devi, Volume 1*" (Chicago: University of Chicago, Department of Anthropology, 1987).

43 The story of Goddess slaying the demon Mahishasura is very popular and is narrated in great detail in Markandeya Purana.

44 Upreti, Mohan; Shah, B. M; written by Shah, B. L. 1952.

45 Myrica esculenta, commonly called Kafal in Pahadi dialect is a small berry like fruit which is available for only short time of the year, during early summers.

46 Budhwar, Kusum. "*Where Gods Dwell*". Penguin Books India, 2010, p. 296.

47 Rawat, Jaisingh. "*Uttarakhand: Janjatiyon ka Itihas*" (Vinasara Pabliśiṅga Kaṃ., 2013)

48 Rāvata, Jayasiṃha.उत्तराखण्ड: जनजातियों का इतिहास. India: Vinasara Pabliśiṅga Kaṃ., 2013.

49 Atkinson, Edwin Thomas. "*The Himalayan Gazetteer, Or, The Himalayan Districts of the North Western Province of India.*" Natraj Publishers, 2014, p. 2631.

50 Mittal, K. Arun, "*British Administration in Kumaon Himalaya*". Mittal Publications, 1986, p.50.

51 Ohri, Lokesh. "*Till Kingdom Come*". State University of New York Press, 2021, p. 416.

52 Ohri, Lokesh. "*Till Kingdom Come*".

53 Dance performances.

54 Walton, H. G. Gazetteer Of Dehradun. India: Natraj Publishers, 1995.

55 Devanagari - थात

56 Christopher D. Wallis, "*Tantra illuminated: The philosophy, history, and practice of a timeless tradition*". Mattamayura Press, 2013.

57 Atkinson, Edwin Thomas. *"The Himalayan Gazetteer."* India: Natraj Publishers, 2014, pg 341.

58 Walton, H. G. Gazetteer Of Dehradun. India: Natraj Publishers, 1995, pg 94.

59 Jones, Mark Gordon. "*Custom, law and John Company in Kumaon.*" (2018).

60 Jones, Mark Gordon. "*Custom, law and John Company in Kumaon.*" 2018.

61 Mittal, Arun K. "*British Administration in Kumaon Himalaya: A Historical Study, 1815-1947*". Mittal Publications, 1986.

62 Atkinson, E. T. "*The Himalayan Gazetteer*".

63 Corbett, Jim. "*The Jim Corbett Omnibus*". OUP India, 1991.

64 Rāya et al.. "*The Mahabharata*", Section 111, Udyoga Parva.

65 Naithani, H. B. "*Floral wealth of Valley of Flowers National Park–A world heritage site–With special reference to Bhundyar valley.*" Uttarakhand Biodiversity Board 433 (2019).

66 Verse 6.74.33 Valmikiramayan.net

67 Sah, Nand K., Shyam Nandan P. Singh, Sudhir Sahdev, Sharmishta Banerji, Vidyanath Jha, Zakir Khan, and Seyed E. Hasnain. "Indian herb 'Sanjeevani'(Selaginella bryopteris) can promote growth and protect against heat shock and apoptotic activities of ultra violet and oxidative stress." *Journal of Biosciences* 30 (2005): 499-505.

68 Dhar, Uppeandra, Ranbeer S. Rawal, and Jyoti Upreti. "*Setting priorities for conservation of medicinal plants—a case study in the Indian Himalaya.*" Biological conservation 95, no. 1 (2000): 57-65.

69 Chen, Steve, Zhaoping Li, Robert Krochmal, Marlon Abrazado, Woosong Kim, and Christopher B. Cooper.

"*Effect of Cs-4®(Cordyceps sinensis) on exercise performance in healthy older subjects: a double-blind, placebo-controlled trial.*" The Journal of alternative and complementary medicine 16, no. 5 (2010): 585-590.

70 Negi, Vikram S., Suresh K. Rana, Lalit Giri, and Ranbeer S. Rawal. "*Caterpillar fungus in the Himalaya, current understanding and future possibilities.*" GB Pant National Institute of Himalayan Environment, Kosi-Katarmal, Almora, Uttarakhand, India Acknowledgements This work is largely based on published literature on caterpillar fungus in Himalaya. We have freely used this information (2020).

71 Negi, Vikram S., Suresh K. Rana, Lalit Giri, and Ranbeer S. Rawal. "*Caterpillar fungus in the Himalaya, current understanding and future possibilities.*" GB Pant National Institute of Himalayan Environment, Kosi-Katarmal, Almora, Uttarakhand, India Acknowledgements This work is largely based on published literature on caterpillar fungus in Himalaya. We have freely used this information (2020).

72 Negi, Vikram S., Suresh K. Rana, Lalit Giri, and Ranbeer S. Rawal. "*Caterpillar fungus in the Himalaya, current understanding and future possibilities.*" GB Pant National Institute of Himalayan Environment, Kosi-Katarmal, Almora, Uttarakhand, India Acknowledgements This work is largely based on published literature on caterpillar fungus in Himalaya. We have freely used this information (2020).

73 Rawat 2005. As shared by Gajendra Singh, scientist, Forestry and Ecology division, Uttarakhand Space Application Center (USAC), Government of Uttarakhand

74 Yadav, Ram R., Krishna G. Misra, Bahadur S. Kotlia, and Neha Upreti. "*Age of Himalayan cedar outside its natural home in the Himalaya.*" Current Science 106, no. 7 (2014): 932-935.

75 Chanchani, Nachiket. "*Mountain temples and temple mountains: architecture, religion, and nature in the Central Himalaya*". University of Washington Press, 2019: Chapter-3

76 Jana, Purna, Kaboli Wotsa, Sabyasachi Dasgupta, and Nagendra P. Todaria. "*Surface water quality in sacred groves of Garhwal Himalayan region, India.*" Current Science (2018): 1105-1110.

77 "*The Unquiet Woods*" by Ramachandra Guha

78 Guha, Ramachandra. "*The Unquiet Woods: ecological change and peasant resistance in the Himalaya*". Univ of California Press, 2000: p. 250.

79 Upadhyay, Vineet. "*Less oak cover in Himalaya could threaten biodiversity: Study.*" New Indian Express. September 5, 2021.

ACKNOWLEDGEMENTS

A heartfelt thanks to Dr. Lokesh Ohri, Convenor, INTACH Uttarakhand Chapter and founder of Been There Doon That, who not only provided valuable insights about the cultures of Uttarakhand but was always available to support and guide.

To Sargam Mehra and Udit Nautiyal, members of Been There Doon That, for helping in research during the early stage of book writing.

To Dr Gajendra Singh, Scientist, Forestry and Ecology division, Uttarakhand Space Application Centre (USAC), for providing beautiful pictures from his personal collection and for enlightening me about the natural diversity of the state.

My sincere gratitude to Prabir Dey of Science Mapping Services for producing the high-quality maps upon request.

To Pooja Saklani, visual designer and head of Mori – a cultural startup, for her beautifully made illustrations and for being the person whom I could rely upon for designing.

I extend my appreciation to the Uttarakhand Tourism Development Board (UTDB) for permitting the use of pictures from their collection.

Anushree Kaushal's line editing transformed the first draft into a masterpiece, ready for the world.

Bhupendra Singh, Head of euttaranchal.com, provided valuable references throughout this book's writing journey.

I would like to thank Sachin Uniyal for volunteering to photograph and breathe visual life into sites I couldn't personally explore.

Cheers to Kevin Missal, CEO of Hubhawks and Vini Bhati, the Publishing Lead at Nu Voice Press, for having faith in my work and giving it a chance to get published.

Abhijeet Kataria's unwavering support and rapid responses throughout the publication journey.

Lastly, the HubHawks team for their seamless, valuable services that eased the entire publication process, making this endeavour truly hassle-free.

Thank you!

ABOUT THE AUTHOR

Neha Mittal is a civil servant of the 2018 batch and posted at the Comptroller and Auditor General of India (CAG)'s office in Uttarakhand. As a skilled storyteller and researcher, she is deeply interested in exploring the various facets of India's classical, regional, and contemporary cultures and their intricate interactions.

Her sojourn with the mountains began with training at the prestigious institutes of LBSNAA in Mussoorie and NAAA in Shimla. Her initial posting in Dehradun allowed her to intimately experience the culture of Uttarakhand, which served as a profound source of motivation for this book.

She is active on her Instagram account: mittaln95.

For more information, you can visit her website: https://nehamittal.in/